# the CHURCH and the SINGLE MOM

## Why You Should Care and What You Can Do

*by*

# Jennifer Barnes Maggio

Published by TLSM Publishing
Baton Rouge, Louisiana 70816
225.341.8055 | www.thelifeofasinglemom.com

Book design copyright © 2020 by TLSM Publishing. All rights reserved.
Cover design by Kedra Deggins

Published in the United States of America

ISBN: 978-1542398961

*Dedication*

*To Healing Place Church for saying yes, your generosity has blessed me beyond words.*

*To the many single moms I've met through the years, what a joy and honor to serve you.*

# PRAISE FOR *THE CHURCH AND THE SINGLE MOM*

"If you do not already have a passion for the single mom, you will! *The Church and the Single Mom* is a genuine look at the state of single parenting across the globe. As I comb through the pages of stories of single moms across the country who have so desperately needed to be cared for and encouraged, my heart yearns to minister to each of them. The necessity to reach single mothers for the cause of Christ transcends age, race, and denomination. And it is exciting to see Jennifer Maggio finally put it on paper!"

**– Nancy Alcorn**
Founder and President of Mercy Multiplied

"This book is a wonderful resource for church leaders. It gives up-to-date statistics and includes vital information about single moms. Excerpts from several single moms' personal struggles helps complete the picture of what single parents go through in attempting to connect with the local church. The book will capture your heart to reach out to single moms. Every church needs it in their leadership library."

**-Linda Ranson Jacobs**
Executive developer of DivorceCare for Kids®
Single parent expert for
the National Center of Biblical Parenting

"Jennifer Maggio is driven by 'holy discontent.' It is not enough that God met her in her own desperate situation as a young unwed mother of two children. It is not enough that the Spirit of God is transforming the lives of hundreds of single moms through the vital and vibrant ministry Jennifer launched and developed in her church, as she learned to step out in faith and follow his lead. Jennifer's 'holy discontent' drives her to prod and poke the sleeping church in America, waking them up to the cries and concerns of myriads of single moms and their families. This is Jennifer's passion and purpose: to provoke and equip the church to reach out effectively to 'the least of these'—those with empty hands who cannot offer anything in return. That is how the church truly begins to love as Jesus did."

— **Carol Floch**
Author of *The Single Moms Devotional*

"Jennifer Maggio succeeds marvelously in giving both individuals and churches and 'insider's' look into the life of a single mom. With heartfelt passion and practical suggestions, her book is overflowing with the resources necessary to make a difference, one mom at a time. Maggio shares her own journey with grace and grit and readers will resonate with her heart that longs to reach out extending hope and love to every single mom. Maggio's enthusiasm is contagious…. Once your read this, there's no going back…. You'll feel compelled to befriend and come alongside every single mom along your path."

— **Michele Howe**
Author of *Going it Alone: Meeting the Challenges of Being a Single Mom* and ten other women's books

"The work of Jennifer Maggio is putting the much-needed hands and feet to the words of our Father who promises to be 'husband to the widow and father to the fatherless.' Too often the single mom and her children are forgotten or ignored by the church. Jennifer brings these precious lives to the forefront while providing practical and compassionate insights into their very difficult life. My prayer is that every single mom would find encouragement through Jennifer's work and every church would be inspired."

**– Dana S. Chisholm**
Author of *Single Moms Raising Sons*

"Exploding the myths shrouding the issue of single moms, an important and timely issue for the church, Jennifer's book is excellent! It challenged me to look beyond the single mom and consider the children, our next generation. As director of one of the nation's busiest pregnancy centers, I witness this epidemic first-hand. These women long for love, acceptance and guidance. Jennifer's compel- ling work demonstrates that offering single moms 'real' love and guidance through Christ and creating practical support and instruction specific to their needs can redirect their path to a life that glorifies God."

**– Pam Caylor**
*Executive director of First Choice*
*Pregnancy Services in Las Vegas, Nevada*

"We've all been waiting for someone to write a book to the church concerning the urgency to reach out to single mothers. This is it! Jennifer Maggio spells out in profound detail how we as the body of Christ must bring help and hope to this growing population. There has never been a greater need to heal our homes and our nation. Every church leader should read this book and take the necessary steps in bringing life into these homes. The time is NOW!"

**-Pam Kanaly**
Co-founder of Survive 'N' Thrive
(a national single parent conference) Author of
*Will the Real Me Please Stand Up?*

"Jennifer Maggio's passion for the single moms is such an inspiration! Her dedication and actions lead the way for so many others to help the multitude of single moms out there."

**– Connie S. Firmin**
Author of *Sparkle: Reflecting Purity in Today's World*

"Jennifer has addressed an international problem at its very core in *The Church and the Single Mom*. There is no way, in good conscience, the church can ignore this issue. I am delighted that someone has written material that is practical and appropriate for all denominations. As one who works with single mothers, I know they come from a wide range of backgrounds with a common thread—the love for their children. Churches should encourage this love by encouraging these moms. This book shows the 'how' and 'why' of working with them. This is a *must read* for every Christian and every church leader."

**-- Gail Cawley Showalter**
Founder of S.M.O.R.E for
Women (Single Mothers Overjoyed, Rejuvenated, and
Empowered)

# CONTENTS

# INTRODUCTION

*I knew we had to do something....*

It all started with one simple article, one thought, one truth—*The Church and the Single Mom*. I had been in ministry for a few years, diligently pursuing my God-given passion for seeing single moms come to a place of full freedom. As my own church became more and more supportive of the ways to serve the single mom, I became increasingly aware that many churches were not quite so aware.

In fact, some were oblivious. Others were indifferent. I knew we had to do something. We had to create an awareness of the hurting around us. The article that follows is what sparked the journey—this global journey of reaching the single mom. The article quickly traveled around the country and was published in magazines and on Web sites before ultimately landing at the Web site of one of the world's largest, most influential ministries—the Christian Broadcasting Network. Read on.

### The Church and the Single Mom

*She walks in the church and cautiously looks around with her four-year-old daughter in tow. She hesitantly makes her way to the back of the church and sits quietly, thumbing through her Bible, avoiding eye contact at all costs. She has contemplated this day for months. She wonders if she should be here. Does she really belong? A warm, friendly woman sits beside her and begins to make conversation with the four-year-old. The young mom is certain the woman notices her empty ring finger and hangs her head in shame.*

*Single moms are one of the fastest-growing sectors of our population, so why have we, the church, ignored them for so long? According to the U.S. Census Bureau's article "Custodial Mothers and Fathers and Their Child Support" released in November 2007, there are more than 13 million across the United States with 27% living in poverty and 24% receiving government assistance. Many of these single moms come from generations of single moms with no hope of breaking this cycle. Currently, 78% percent of our prison population come from a single parent home, according to the Index of Leading Cultural Indicators. A new study released in March 2007 by University of Pennsylvania's School of Medicine found that almost 50% percent of single-parent homes have some form of sexual abuse.*

*Is it any wonder that 22% of all pregnancies today end in abortion (Guttmacher Institute, July 2008)?! Potential single mothers are fearful that they simply cannot parent alone. They are scared—overwhelmed with the idea. Where are the resources for single moms? Where can they go? Sure, there are government pro- grams to put food in the mouths of her hungry children, but what about her emotional state? Where does she go for friendship and networking? How does she achieve financial success? Does she know the resources that are available to her, other than government assistance?*

*For far too long the church has run from the single mom. Don't believe me? Some studies suggest that as many as 67% of single moms currently do not attend church—many citing fear of being judged as key. Of course, we offer them food when they are hungry. We may occasionally perform a home repair or provide toys at Christmas. But do we stop there? Dare we open a Sunday school class exclusively for single moms? A Bible study? Or even a full-scale ministry?*

*It seems that many churches fear what others may perceive about a single moms ministry. We know that God meant for marriage to be forever (Malachi 2:16, Genesis 2:24, Matthew 19:8). We also know that our God commands sexual purity (1 Corinthians 6:18, 1 Corinthians 6:13, Galatians 5:19). Does ministering to single moms mean that we, as the church, condone unwed pregnancy or divorce? Of course not—no more than drug rehabilitation programs support drug use.*

*If we don't reach out to them, who will? For many, the only counseling they receive is from the local government-run health unit, where they simply receive a pat on the back and a safe-sex discussion. Are you okay with these precious moms receiving a condom, or should we be giving them Christ? How can they make it without Christ filling them and renewing them daily? How do they not simply give up?*

*As Christians, we have been commissioned with several tasks by our Heavenly Father. Psalm 146:9 says "He cares for the widows and orphans." Luke 14:13 calls us to "invite the poor." 1 Timothy 5:3 advises us to "take care of the widow." The widow, oftentimes, is the single mom. The orphans are left by a single mom. The poor are the single moms.*

*As a former unwed teen mom, I can tell you that 15 years ago when I began the journey, there was nothing for single moms at the local church. I was ashamed and fell away from church attendance. For almost seven years, I hung my head in shame.*

*Whether they are unwed or divorced, many single moms need parenting advice, financial instruction, emotional support via networking, and Spiritual growth opportunities. Let us find these women in our communities, both the churched and the unchurched. Let us minister to them at their point of need. Let's begin single moms groups. Praise God for the cutting-edge churches across the country who have already embraced the concept! Has yours?*

You see, ministry isn't ministry just because it has a good book or article behind it. What does the writing represent? What are you **doing**? Faith without works is dead....

## CHAPTER 1

# WHY WOULD I CARE?

*I am happily married with three beautiful children,*
*but let me share a little of how it used to be.*

T he single mom. The hurting, broken divorcée. The sweet teenage girl who finds herself in an impossible situation. You may wonder why in the world I would care about the single-parent epidemic. I am happily married with three beautiful children. I have a picture-perfect life with a loving husband, a successful career, and a typical middle-class income. Everything in my life is pretty neat, clean, and comfortable. Let me share a little of how it used to be.

*It was late in the night, I suspect well past midnight, when I heard a great deal of commotion coming from the kitchen. I staggered out of bed and grabbed my favorite blanket (at only three years old, I didn't go anywhere without it). I rubbed my eyes and headed sleepily down the long, dark hallway to see what was going on. To my shock, I found my drunk father leaning over the kitchen sink covered in blood. My step-mother was washing blood from his face and head. I stood there in horror. It was not long before I was noticed and quickly ushered back to my bed. I was then left alone in my dark bedroom ... horrified that my daddy may be bleeding to death.*

*This is my earliest memory.*

*I later discovered that my father had been driving drunk and drove his 1978 Chevrolet pick-up truck into a ravine, smashing the windshield and his head. Surprisingly, he managed to drive the truck home and was in desperate need of medical care. My stepmother, fearing there would be legal trouble for his drunk-driving, washed him off and provided the best care she could. I would love to tell you this was some rare, one-time event of craziness in my life, but I can't.*

*At three years old, my life was already in complete turmoil. Just over a year earlier, my mother, who played piano for our local church, loaded my twin sister and me into the family car and began the short trek to church for Sunday service. We backed down the driveway and no sooner had we driven a few feet down the road than we were we struck head-on by a speeding 15-year-old drunk driver. He was just coming in from partying the night before and, in an instant, my mother was killed.*

*My dad was not with us that morning. In fact, he was deer hunting alone. He was listening to the local radio station when he heard about a car wreck near our home in which a 32-year-old woman had been killed. He rushed home with a sick feeling in his stomach. As he encountered the scene, his fears were confirmed—his beautiful young wife was dead. What was he going to do? He had twin baby daughters just over a year old. His world spiraled out of control.*

*My dad had already been married once and lost that wife to an ugly divorce. He later watched their 17-year-old son die a slow, painful death due to heart problems. My dad had already suffered a lifetime of pain and now he was staring into the face of his future—now gone. All hope for a happy ending was gone. He sought his comfort in the bottom of a beer bottle, and it was many years later before I saw my dad without a beer in his hand.*

*My dad was an angry drunk. When he consumed alcohol he became mean and violent. Anyone who wronged him would hear about it during one of his drunken frenzies. This was the case the night he stood at the end of our driveway with his pistol drawn screaming profanities at my uncle who lived across the street. My uncle, in turn, stood at the end of his driveway with his pistol in hand. This standoff lasted for some time as I watched through my bedroom window, fearing my daddy would be killed.*

*During the drinking years, if he wasn't pulling a gun on someone, it was always something else. He would get into a vehicle drunk—even after my mother was killed—and drive around our yard, gouging huge circles and ruts in the yard. He screamed and threw furniture. He shouted obscenities regularly. He called long-lost relatives just to give them a good cussing out. He would disappear and came home late at night, usually with a new girlfriend.*

*It was not long after my mother's death that my dad remarried, bringing wife number three into our home. Barbara had no children of her own. My dad later shared with me that he married so quickly in order to have a caretaker for his twin baby girls. He needed help. He needed to work and provide for us and had no one, so ... he found a wife. What my dad did not know was that Barbara was no "gem." She beat me and would lock me in a dark closet for punishment. She didn't feed me regularly and made me wear clothes so tight they cut*

*off my circulation. Some mother she was!*

When I look back, I can recall only bits and pieces of my childhood. Some of it is a blur, while other incidents are as clear as if they happened this morning.

At some point not long thereafter, Daddy divorced Barbara and ushered in wife number four—Francis. I don't remember much about Francis. I do remember that I liked her and she was most-often kind to me. Our new Momma brought with her a teenage son, John. It was not long before John was left to care for me while our parents went out. He began molesting me, and I can even remember him doing it while onlookers watched. We never discussed it. It was a secret I kept hidden for many years. Daddy and "Momma Francis" would go to dinner and leave us under the care of neighbors as well. It was during this time that our next-door neighbor's teenage son joined in the "fun." He, too, began to molest me on different occasions.

Along with living through molestation and abuse and the toll it was taking on me, I watched Daddy's marriage to Francis end through infidelity. There was so much I did not understand. Nothing in my life was secure.

It seemed that one day Francis was moving out and the very next wife number five was moving in! Wife number five was Candy, and she was one of the worst! She seemed nice enough at first. I was about eight years old when Candy came into my life. She brought three children of her own to the marriage, all roughly the same age as my twin sister and me. She had a special needs son who suffered from some form of mental retardation and had to be cared for around the clock. This quickly became the children's job, and so we were often *left feeding, bathing, and changing the diapers of a boy who was our same age. Candy was much younger than my father and you could certainly tell. She had a jealous streak and was very immature. Many unspeakable things took place in my home. Some were so horrific that I could never share them. Most people could not handle reading them.*

*My dad worked away for extended periods of time, so I was left alone in the "care" of Candy. She could be kind, loving, and caring one moment, and in the next snap into a fury of rage because I hadn't folded the towels or cleaned the bathroom properly ... or any other of a long list of chores she deemed appropriate for an eight-year-old girl. One minute she was sneaking boys over to our home behind my father's back and the next we would be beaten for even allowing a boy to call us on the phone! I now look back and wonder if she suffered from some type of mental illness—maybe bipolar disorder. It's just a thought.*

*When Candy was mean, she was scary. She would hold me against the wall choking me to the point that I was sure I would pass out. She beat me with the belt many times, leaving welts and bruises. She screamed vile, awful profanities at me and plunged my self-esteem to an all-time low. In her fits of rage she told me she would kill me. She even went so far as to force me to watch pornography at a young age. I remember sitting in our living room watching the filth, not even sure of what I was watching. As time went on, I would cry and leave the room. At times she would actually come get me and make me watch it. I get nauseated even writing about the filth that she shoved into my young mind.*

*Candy made us do many immoral things. Unbeknownst to my father she would take us shopping at department stores.*

*She put things on a layaway payment plan and would purchase things for us, even when finances were extremely tight. Returned checks came in the mail almost daily, and Candy was certain to check the mail before my father came home. She had us lie to him. She had us steal newspapers out of neighbors' yards instead of getting our own subscription. We would steal yard art from other neighborhoods instead of purchasing our own.*

*We were officially white trash. I knew it and I hated it.*

*My step-grandfather also began molesting me while my dad was married to Candy. I had already been down that road before with others in my life and knew the drill: I needed to keep my mouth shut. What if someone didn't believe me when I told? I was sick. I was scared. I was humiliated and embarrassed. I feared that if so much as breathed a word to a soul I would be punished severely. I regret now that I didn't speak up sooner, for fear that there were many others in that family who were also taken advantage of by that man.*

*Through it all, though, I loved each one of my stepmothers —Candy included. Each one temporarily filled a void in my life. They acted as Mother, if only for a while. Even when times were bad, I think I always hoped that one marriage, one girlfriend, would last. They never did. Infidelity crept into my dad's marriage to Candy, too. And after a few years of marriage, she was gone. The divorce was just as ugly as the marriage.*

*My parents often pitted the children against each other. At the end of their marriage, they fought—physically threw punches—constantly. Even after they separated, I lived in fear that Candy would come to our house and beat me or fight with my dad. There was a huge sigh of relief when they divorced, yet still, deep within me, I mourned the loss of yet another mother.*

*During the next six months, my dad moved through two girl-friends. He did not pay much attention to me, so I began a new path—that of teenage sex. I was 13 years old and tended to hang around kids much older than I was. I began sneaking out of the house and drinking alcohol on weekends. I lied regarding my whereabouts, and my dad was too busy dating to notice. I had avoided the peer pressure of having sex for some years, but here I was at 13 years old embarking on that journey. My first sexual encounter was with a much older boy. I only did it to keep him dating me, to keep him "interested." I didn't even want to. But I didn't stand up for myself and express that, and in just a few moments I had given away a precious gift of purity to someone who surely did not know or care. The relationship ended only a few weeks later, and I was devastated.*

*Thus began a pattern of giving myself away sexually to various young men whom I was certain loved me and thought I was special. I was in a desperate search for validation in life, desperate for someone to love me for me. I wanted all the past hurt to go away. I wanted all the years of disappointment, pain, and loss to disappear. The only things that disappeared were my self-respect and self-esteem. I was left with a huge void within me. I was ashamed and embarrassed, but I didn't stop.*

*As you may have guessed, it was time for my dad to remarry— again! Wife number six was Mary. She was a different creature altogether. She was the most evil of all the stepmothers, the most abusive, the most unkind. Their marriage started off, as most of them had, with the new stepmother's being very kind to me. She pretended to value my thoughts and spent time with me. Only a few weeks into the marriage, though, all that changed. It was painfully obvious that she resented having children in the home and was on a mission to make our lives miserable. Mary had three grown children and had not raised any of them. They were raised by their father, Mary's ex-husband. She loathed children and counted down the days until I graduated. I entered my high school years with my home life as tumultuous as ever. I continued to lie and sneak around. And I met my high school sweetheart.*

*From the moment I laid eyes on Dillon, I just knew that we would be together forever. I was playing high school basketball. He was the star of the boys' basketball team. He was tall, dark, and handsome. He was extremely charismatic and all the girls liked him. And ... he liked me. I could hardly believe it! I hung on his every word. My dad hated all my boyfriends and this one would be no different. Well ... except for one major detail....*

*He was black.*

*My dad was born in rural Mississippi in 1935, and albeit a flimsy excuse, he was born during a time and in a place where interracial dating was frowned upon, to say the least. The fact that Dillon was black peeled back yet another layer of anger in my father, and it was quite exciting to me. My dad did not like it and I did not care. I had found my Romeo.*

*During the next seven years I was nearly obsessed with Dillon. We sneaked around to see each other as often as possible. He made me feel like a million bucks—at first. He complimented me regularly. "You are so beautiful. You have the prettiest eyes. I love your long brown hair." All the perfect things I needed to hear to fill my empty self-esteem tank. Before long, this relationship turned sexual. And not* long after I discovered that I was not Dillon's only Juliet. In fact, there were at least a dozen Juliets. Dillon's charm penetrated right to the heart of many young women in our high school and he took full advantage of it. He had many girlfriends during our seven-year relationship.

The additional girlfriends were not our only problem. I was 15 years old and a sophomore in high school the first time Dillon pulled my hair. I was speaking with another boy at school. Dillon saw it and did not like it. He came to my house that night, as he often did, and I sneaked him in. He grabbed me very tightly by the hair, pulling me close to him, and whispered in my ear that I had better not talk to that guy again. He explained to me how he felt about me talking to other boys. Though he did not really hurt me that night, after he left my house I wondered what had just happened. I was scared and confused. That began years of hair-pulling, pushing, shoving, and physical violence that kept me in fear of him.

Physical abuse and infidelity were only part of the story. He also abused me mentally and emotionally. Early on in the relationship, compliments flowed. He treated me like a princess. That abruptly stopped. I hated it. He began giving me the cold shoulder very often and ignored me at school. I was his night-time lover and his day-time reject. But since I had given myself over to him physically I felt an emotional attachment to him and could not—or rather would not—let him go. Compliments gave way to insults and put-downs. He would comment that he did not like the outfit I wore to school that day or how I fixed my hair. Whatever the insult, it stung and burned deep within me. He tore me down, only to build me up later that night, in secret, behind closed doors.

The question now arises: "Why in the world would you stay with someone who treated you like that? Multiple girlfriends?

*Abuse? Why?!"*

*It had nothing to do with intelligence. I was a straight-A student who later graduated high school valedictorian. I was on the homecoming court. I was Class President. It was not as if I was too dumb to figure out what was going on. It was never a head issue. It was always a heart issue. Think about my life for a moment. My mother was killed. My dad was an alcoholic. I had a barrage of stepmothers who beat me, malnourished me, forced me to steal, and forced me to view pornography. I was molested time and again. I was an emotional wreck. I NEEDED this relationship to work. No matter how twisted it seemed, I needed Dillon to love me.*

*I became pregnant twice by Dillon in high school and miscarried both times. The summer before my senior year, I decided that I would move on with my life, graduate, and begin a successful college career far away from my existing life. I would leave Dillon behind. That resolve didn't last. Only a few weeks into our senior year, we got back together. Within months, I found myself pregnant a third time. I hid that pregnancy through graduation in 1995. I graduated high school in May, turned 18 in June, and informed my father that I was about six months pregnant. His exact words to me were, "Have a nice life!"*

*I was devastated.*

*Dillon received a basketball scholarship and, by summer's end, would be going to college several hours away, leaving me behind to fend for myself. I was now homeless. I was not permitted to get my clothes from the family home, had nowhere to go, and no future. Even as I sit and write to you about my journey, several years later, tears come to my eyes when I think of the sheer loneliness and desperation I felt.*

*The loneliness and desperation only escalated when the news came that Dillon had another baby on the way. As if that weren't bad enough, he had chosen to marry the girl! The horror! The shock! This was the absolute worst possible scenario. Not only had I lost my whole family and most of my friends, but I had now lost the one person I felt certain I was destined to be with, the one I was sure loved me as much as I loved him. My life was over. I cried out "Why?! Why?! Why?!" I screamed frantically. I shouted at the top of my lungs. Why? Why was my life such a mess? Why was I all alone? How could this have happened to me? It was the closest I ever came to suicide.*

*I bounced around from house to house for a while, staying with friends. I was unsure of exactly where I would go when an angel stepped in to help—Becky Chapman. Becky was the mother of a good high school friend. Becky's daughter and I had been friends for many years and I knew the family well. The Chapmans stepped up to the plate and offered me and my unborn child a place to stay. For that, I was—and am—eternally grateful. Becky helped me get prenatal care (I was seven months pregnant by this time), government assistance, college enrollment, and housing plans. She was an ear when I needed to talk. She treated me like family. She was the mother I never had.*

*Within a few short weeks, I was lying in a hospital bed holding my precious newborn son, after over 20 hours of labor. As I looked into his big brown eyes, tears began rolling down my face as the reality of my "aloneness" just set in. There was no one to ask about how to raise this son. I didn't have a mother to offer wise counsel. I knew my baby did not deserve the life I was bringing him into. I knew he was innocent and precious. I vowed that I would never allow him to experience the things I had. I was going to be a good mother. I brought him home from the hospital and, just 10 days later, I went to work for the first time. I was a waitress* *at a local pizza parlor. I received news that I qualified for government housing and moved into the local government subsidized housing project. Slowly, friends began to donate furniture and household goods to me. Through the generosity of my aunt I was able to purchase my first car (for $600). I enrolled in college at night, worked full-time during the day, and cared for my newborn son, alone. Within a few months, I had landed a better job and could finally see a light at the end of the tunnel. It was not the life I had planned for myself, but I was making it. I was surviving.*

*Dillon came home from college on a break. And then ... I got pregnant again. There is no way—simply no way—to adequately describe the humiliation and shame that fell upon me. Was I a glutton for punishment? Was I determined to sabotage my future happiness? What was I thinking? I mean, he had married another girl! Was I completely crazy?! I sure felt that way! I was 19 years old and pregnant for a fourth time. I could not afford to care for one child, much less two.*

*Thus, I began the difficult task of hiding yet another pregnancy. I hid the pregnancy from **everyone** until the latter stages. About seven months into my pregnancy, I finally told my boss, my family, and my friends. You can imagine the things they said to me. The truth is, there was nothing anyone could say to me that I had not already said to myself—and then some.*

*I gave birth to an almost nine-pound baby girl in June 1997. I welcomed her home on a Friday and was back at work on Monday. I had no choice. There was no sick pay. There was no vacation time. If I did not work, then my children did not eat. It was that simple. I did what I had to do. I dropped out of college, continued to work full-time during the day, and rarely slept. I was up most nights with at least one of my children. Having two children under the age of two is difficult for any parent, but especially for a single teen mom.*

*Dillon soon graduated from college, divorced his wife, and moved back home. We continued our relationship. It was not ideal, to say the least. The relationship was still marked with countless episodes of infidelity. When I got home from work, I often didn't know where Dillon was. He disappeared for days on end. He rarely held down a job. He smoked marijuana. He abused me both physically and mentally on a regular basis. Yet, in some way, I continued to romanticize the relationship to be some type of Romeo-Juliet love story, where against all odds we would ultimately be together. I excused Dillon's behavior. He was just young and immature, "but, someday ... someday, we would live happily ever after." One night, after a particularly explosive argument over yet another female interest in his life, Dillon left in a fit of anger after trashing my apartment. That did it. I had had it. I fell to my knees on the bathroom floor of my tiny apartment and wept. I cried out. I placed my face on that cold bathroom floor and cried for what seemed like an eternity.*

*A thousand questions swarmed through my head. Was this all life had to offer? When would this pain and agony end? I was living in government housing on food stamps and welfare. I drove a beat-up 15-year-old car that left me stranded regularly on the side of the road. I had no money, a dead-end job, and a dead-end relationship. It seemed more than I could possibly bear. As I lay there crying hysterically, my young son walked into the bathroom, put his arms around me, and began to say, "It's otay, Mommy. It's otay."*

*It was in that moment that I realized that I was giving my children the same life I had suffered. The abuse, anger, financial hardship, and instability had now become part of their lives, too. Things in my life could not have gotten much worse....*

*Therefore, at the urging of my sweet sister, I went back to church.*

Let me stop the story for one moment. I am about to tell you something that may shock you. There was never a period of time in my childhood when I did not attend church. You heard me. *Never.* Every Sunday, my family got up, dressed in our Sunday best, and put on a happy face for the whole church. There were periods of time when my father did not attend church with us, but even on those occasions he always took my sister and me to church and dropped us off. I could quote scripture backwards and forwards. I knew the basic foundation of Christianity and even accepted Christ as my Savior when I was nine years old. In the midst of all the turmoil and abuse, he was my only solace.

During the early years of my Christianity, I did lean on Jesus. I went to church two to three times a week. I read my Bible daily and prayed regularly. Jesus was my best friend. There was joy in my heart. By the time I was 12, I left Jesus behind for raging hormones and boys. It was then that I started "pretending" church. I attended regularly through my high school years. I even participated in a few youth group events, but my heart was rarely in it. I was ashamed of my home life. I was ashamed of my mistakes. I never quite felt that I measured up to the other kids who were there. After getting pregnant with my son, I fell away from church completely.

Back to the story.

*The morning after that bathroom floor incident, I found myself getting ready for church. It had been years since I had been in church. I was nervous. I felt the weight of the world on my shoulders. I had to make myself drive to church and get out. I had a dozen excuses for why I should not have been there. I got out of my car, unloaded my two children, and made it just inside the church and sat on the back row. I was certain that the whole church was staring at me. I was certain that a spotlight would soon shine a bright light down upon me and I would be ridiculed and mocked for my oh-so-obvious sins, or that lightning would strike me down. I sat silently on the back row and don't remember anyone even saying "hello."*

*I would like to be able to tell you that my glorious return to church that day turned into some miracle moment, whereby my whole life changed, and I lived happily ever after. It did not. I did, however, resolve to go back again. Before long, I found myself attending church regularly. It was a difficult process. I went to a small church. I was in my early 20s, had two children, and was unmarried. What Sunday School class would I join? The Adult class had no one younger than 40. The youth class had teens and college-aged kids, but they certainly did not have children. Where did I fit in? I struggled with that one for months. Nonetheless, I continued going.*

*After attending for some time, one Sunday the pastor began preaching a sermon on "the tithe." For those who are unfamiliar with this principle, tithe simply means "tenth." It is the teaching that believers are to give 10% of their earnings to the church. As I sat in my seat, I began to smile. "You are kidding, right? Give money to the church? I'm broke. I can barely afford to feed my children. I'm rubbing pennies together to put gas in my car!"*

*These were my thoughts. I even considered, "The pastor must need a new car. That is what this is all about." Try as I might, I could not get the sermon out of my head. Months passed, and after much consideration, I was certain that God must be dealing with me on this topic because I could not forget it. That next Sunday I resolved to start tithing.*

*It was weird, at first. Nothing changed. I was still financially destitute. I still received food stamps and welfare. I still lived in government housing. But, as with church attendance, I decided to be obedient and continue to do it. If I was going to really give this church thing a try, I had to be all in. My first tithe check was about*
*$35. I was making $350 per month through my employer. Within six months of my first tithe check, I landed a new job that earned me three times more income monthly. It wasn't a gold mine, but it sure was nice to begin to do more than just scrape by!*

*As I continued on my trek with church, I was struggling internally. I was still in and out of a relationship with Dillon. I still had sex with him outside marriage. I still went out to the local bars, occasionally, and drank. I was not perfect. My spirit was at war— the battle of good and evil. Honestly, I stayed in limbo for some time thereafter, straddling the fence with one foot in church and the other in the things of the world. But God is always faithful. I did continue to attend church regularly. I did continue to tithe faithfully. I became discontent with this seven-year dead-end relationship. It had dragged on long enough.*

*Miraculously, I was offered a job in Corporate America— a job I hadn't been looking for and was not completely qualified for. A gentleman had approached my boss and explained that he was currently looking to fill a position in his company. My boss, who thought very highly of me, told me about the opportunity and suggested that I go for an interview. What evidence of God's divine favor on my life! Not only did I have an existing boss who thought so highly of me that he would help me obtain a better job, but I landed that job that, by all accounts, I was not qualified to get.*

*I worked in that corporate job for almost 10 years and became one of the most well-recognized executives in the region. I went on to earn a six-figure salary, got off government assistance, bought my own home, and was finally able to provide financially for my children! What a testament to how God's hand works in our lives!*

*To bring my story full-circle, I will tell you that I went on to leave that dead-end seven-year relationship with Dillon behind. God slowly gave me the strength and courage I needed to move on. He gradually changed my heart so that I no longer needed nor desired my past life. Only after I became emotionally healthy and whole in who I was in Christ did he later bring me a husband, Jeff. Jeff is one of the sweetest Christian men I have ever met. We fell in love, married, and he adopted my two children. We now share a third child together.*

*My story is not about how tithing mysteriously earns you a six-figure income. (I do not insinuate that at all.) My story is not about how I survived abuse and poverty. Ultimately my story is about God's faithfulness— his overwhelming love for his children and his willingness to reach down and pluck us out of an eternal separation. My story is one of how my commitment to obedience resulted in God's further blessing upon my life.*

When the Lord called me into full-time ministry, I ignored the calling. I felt so ill-equipped. I was happy in my corporate job. I was successful and comfortable. For nearly a year, the thought that recurred deep within my soul was that I was to leave Corporate America and begin to minister to single moms. As I finally found the courage to walk away from my stable income and my comfort zone and into the purposes of God, I found a rich blessing—the blessing of ministry.

You see, although my life was comfortable and I had found great freedom in Christ, I never forgot those moments of despair. I have never forgotten how I felt the first time I re-entered the church. I have never forgotten the shame, humiliation, and the embarrassment of having multiple unplanned pregnancies and the shameful publicity of it all. As I delved deeper into ministry, I could counsel with these single moms and hurting women on a deeper level, for I had been there. I had felt the pain.

As easy as it would be to believe that my story is merely a tragic rarity, it is not. Not only can you clearly read the statistics that support single parents and abuse, poverty, high crime, and low education, but if you seek, you will surely find the single moms in your own community. And you most certainly will not have to search long, for they are everywhere.

CHAPTER 2

# WHAT IN THE WORLD IS GOING ON?

*It is safe to say that we have an epidemic on our hands.*

Maybe you think my story is a rarity, a one-off, a sad tale. As tragic as my own story is, however, it pales in comparison with the stories of many with whom I have counseled over the years. As heart-breaking as my story is, it has a happy ending. Many of the single-parenting stories being lived out across this country do not end quite so well. Let me paint a picture for you.

In 1951, approximately 22% of the United States population lived in a single-parent home. By 2018, that number had risen to 35%. Further, there are approximately 23 million single-parent homes in the United States. (Annie E. Case Foundation, Kids Count Data, 2018). According to Pew Research Center, nearly 65% of babies are born into a single-parent homes (2018). A baby is more likely to be born outside marriage than within. While divorce rates have fallen to 36%, this is only due to couples choosing to cohabitate versus marry (CDC/NCHS National Vital

Statistics System, 2018).

It is safe to say that we have an epidemic on our hands. Poverty. Abuse. Delinquency. Crime. Imprisonment. Under-education. All are major issues related to single parenting.

## POVERTY

According to the U.S. Census Bureau, of the households headed by single mothers in 2018, 39% lived below the poverty line, with the average income of these families totaling $32,000 annually. Approximately 42% of all children living in single-parent home are poor. Children in poverty are much more likely to experience violence, chronic neglect, and accumulated burdens, culminating into stress response and difficulties in learning and memory function, according to findings in the Heritage Foundation Family Facts Study (*2010).*

Because educational underachievement is an ongoing issue in single-parent homes, the plight of poverty within this sector of the population is likely to persist without drastic change. Although single mothers are often cited as working multiple jobs to make ends meet, many times they can still only obtain minimum-wage or low wage-earning positions. On average, the United States pays out $80 billion in welfare assistance to single-parent households each year. 16% of single-parent homes are forced to use government assistance, resulting in an estimated $500 billion to be paid out in welfare to needy families each year. While 16% may seem like a low number, this is a direct result of the poverty threshold being increased, leaving many families without the ability to receive assistance. (U.S. Government Publishing Office 2019 & US Bureau of Labor and Statistics, 2018).

## ABUSE

In the fourth National Incidence Study of Child Abuse and Neglect, Congressional Report from 2010, the rate of child abuse in single-parent households is 21%, compared to 8% in two-parent households, almost triple. This same study found that children in fatherless homes were:

- 71% more likely to be maltreated
- 62% more likely to be neglected
- 59% more likely to sustain serious physical injury from abuse

Further, in the 2011-2012 National Survey of Children's Health, 21 percent of children cared for by a divorced or separated mother had lived with someone—usually a parent or sibling—who "had a problem with alcohol or drugs." This was five times higher than the rate for children cared for by married birth parents, which was 4 percent. Fifteen percent of kids with a divorced or separated mother had lived with someone "who was mentally ill or suicidal, or severely depressed for more than a couple of weeks." This was triple the rate for children in intact families.

Correspondingly, the U.S Department of Health and Human Services reports that in 2014, 1.4 million children resided in a single parent household that abused alcohol. 39% of men that have admitted to being sexually abused, shared that they grew up in a single parent home (Center for Health Equity Research and Promotion, 2007) It is also estimated that seventy-five percent of adolescent patients in chemical abuse treatment come from fatherless homes.

## IMPRISONMENT AND CRIME

Single-parent households account for 90% of the increase in crime rates between 1973 and 1995 (Dwayne Garrett, Content for

Re- print). Further, children from fatherless homes are:

- 85% more likely to exhibit a behavioral dysfunction (Center for Disease Control, 2018)
- 80% more likely to have displaced anger leading them to become rapists (Criminal Justice & Behavior, Vol 14, p. 403-26, 1978)
- 70% more likely to become juvenile delinquents (U.S. Dept. of Justice, Special Report, 2014)
- 85% more likely to become part of the prison population (Texas Department of Corrections, 2018)

Prison inmates' children are also twice as likely to commit a crime, thus creating generations of single-parent households (Aggression and Violent Behavior Journal, 2017).

## EDUCATION

According to a National Principals Association report on the State of High Schools, 71% of all high school dropouts come from a fatherless home, leaving these children 9 times more likely to drop out of high school. College attendance is significantly lower as well.

The U.S. Census Bureau Report in 2016 stated that 17 million children live with a single mom. This leaves single mom households as the second largest family group in the nation. What type of future can these children look forward to? Nationally children from fatherless homes are:

- 5 times more likely to commit suicide (U.S. D.H.H.S., Bureau of the Census, Juvenile Delinquency, Crime, and Gangs, 2020)
- 32 times more likely to run away (U.S. D.H.H.S., Bureau of the Census, 2020)
- 20 times more likely to have behavioral dysfunction (U.S. D.H.H.S., Bureau of the Census, 2020)

- 10 times more likely to use drugs or alcohol (Rainbows for all God's Children, 2020)
- 20 times more likely to end up in prison (Texas Dept. of Corrections, 2018)

Based on my counseling of hundreds of single-parent families I can attest to the state of the next generation of children from single-mother homes. I have seen a significant number of pre-adolescent and adolescent children with behavioral problems. Many of them even consider suicide as a viable option for their futures. Many children in single-parent homes have had a front-row seat at their parents' malicious divorce and nasty custody battle. Others have an absentee father. In nearly every case—no matter what the circumstances—these children tend to blame themselves for the turmoil in their family life. They feel their security has been jeopardized.

There is no doubt that single mothers are among the hardest working people in our country. They often serve as mother and father. They tend to all the household duties. They act as chauffeur, maid, and counselor. They work two jobs or go to school—or both. They budget and plan for their children's future. They are the unsung heroes of our day. Many are shattering glass ceilings and eradicating poor statistical data in their homes.

Is it any wonder that she is exhausted and overwhelmed?

This is not simply an American problem; it is a global problem. An epidemic that cuts across racial, ethnic, and national boundaries. The plight of single-parenthood with all of its challenges is a global phenomenon. According to the Pew Research center, in 2019 single parent homes are an increasing norm across the globe with the following percentages in various countries.

- United Kingdom—21%
- Ireland—14%
- Sao Tome a Principe 19%
- Uganda 10%
- Kenya 16%
- Nigeria 4%
- Germany—12%
- Russia – 18%
- France – 16%
- Canada 14%
- Mexico – 7%

## A Pop Culture Sensation?

It seems that pop culture has become fascinated with teen pregnancy and single-parenting. In 2009, MTV launched *16 and Pregnant*. The show enjoyed such popularity and high ratings that the network eventually launched *Teen Mom* and *Teen Mom 2*. These reality shows continue to rank among the highest-rated shows on MTV. MTV has received both critical acclaim for the programs and scathing scrutiny and criticism. What I am about to say may shock you: I, a conservative, church-going, radical Jesus freak is an avid viewer of the program!

I do not confess to know the motive behind MTV's launch of these programs. While I would love to believe that it was solely for the increased awareness and protection of our next generation, I rather doubt it. Whatever the reason, the fact remains that these programs do, in fact, create awareness among our teen and young adult population about the "reality" of teenage motherhood. Having worked full-time with single mothers of all types—teen moms, divorcées, and widows—I am passionate about bringing awareness to single-parent issues. While MTV chronicles only the lives of teen moms, it does expose the raw truth of parenting alone.

When I first began viewing the show, I could not make it through any episode without breaking down in tears. The reality of what I had lived through (and millions like me) bled through every show. The humiliation of an unexpected pregnancy quickly faded, and the hope of a future marriage to my child's father blossomed. Before long the relationship would fall apart and reality would set in. The same story is played out in nearly every episode, thus creating a keen awareness that even in the young minds of teenagers who secretly hope to have the white picket fence and a Prince Charming, the reality inevitably is vastly different.

My biggest concern about the program is that it lacks to provide any real help. Creating awareness, as important as it is, is only the first step in problem-solving. The women featured on the program are in need of resources—not simply financial resources but counseling and spiritual guidance. I am curious to know how much of the millions of dollars the wildly popular show has generated has been spent on financial education, parenting classes, and counseling for these young girls whose stories bring such stellar ratings.

Each episode of *16 and Pregnant* ends with a personal video interview of the young teen mom. As she chronicles her own journey, she always—without fail—says that she wishes she had waited. She confesses that she had no idea how hard it would be. Crushing. Heart-breaking. *Real.*

What about Hollywood? Single parenting has become the norm for many leading ladies. While the wealth of these single moms certainly alleviates the financial burden that other single moms face, it does not compensate for the lack of stability that most single-parented children experience. The public feuding over custody and who's fault the failed relationship is—often played out on the cover of tabloids—undoubtedly alters the future emotional health of the children involved.

## Where all these numbers lead…

There you have it—a quick glimpse of the state of the union, the state of our global union. I am exasperated even sharing these statistics with you. With tears in my eyes, the passion the Lord birth- ed within me to minister to single moms burns inside me— even deeper, even brighter. What is it that we, the church, are supposed to do about the problem? How can we sit idly by and watch the future of our next generation crumble?

Please don't misunderstand me. I am not saying that there are not exceptions to this bleak reality I have shared in this chapter. There are single mothers all across this land who have successfully reared their children and gone on to live happy, healthy lives. There are women who are serving the Lord, parenting alone, and waiting on God patiently to move them into their next season of life.

But exceptions prove the rule: the statistics are true. They glare before us. And the shining beacon of hope—the *only* hope—is that our Heavenly Father is far more powerful than any statistic. The church—the hands and feet and heart of Christ—can and should get active, get prepared, and be willing to radically change the lives of these precious families.

Now you know why I care. I can only hope and pray that you understand why you should, too. *But what can we do?*

CHAPTER 3

# RESPONSIBILITY

*What does the plight of the single mom have to do with us—the church—and with you—the Christian?*

Y ou now understand what is happening around the globe. You know my story and why God has birthed this enormous passion within me. But what does any of that have to do with us—the church—and with you, the Christian?

In our day, there is an ever-increasing awareness of social justice—and rightly so. I believe that every Christian has a God given passion. There is that "something" inside of us that we *must* do. What is this *something* inside of you? Helping the homeless? Orphans? Widows? Home or foreign missions? Anti-abortion advocacy? Helping abuse victims? Helping to liberate those enslaved in human trafficking?

Do you realize that every issue listed here commonly affects the single-parent family, either directly or indirectly?

When I spoke with a church leader in a neighboring state recently about starting a single moms ministry, his response was:

"We simply do not have many single moms in our congregation…. So we do not see the need to start such a program."

I began to cry out to the Lord in frustration, "Why don't **they** get it, Lord?!" I felt an immediate response in my spirit, "Because you do    " I decided right then that rather than being frustrated because every leader did not see this as clearly as I did, my fire was fueled to actively do something about it. "Wow." I was stunned. I was simply stunned.

## Called to reach the "missing" 70%

*Isn't that the problem?* When we hear that nearly 70% of single mothers in our country do not actively attend church (many citing fear and shame as reasons), does that not mean that we are to be actively searching for these single parents? We as the church in our day have a duty to be the hands and feet of Jesus. The need is urgent, especially in light of the sweeping changes that have rock- ed the very foundation of our society—the family unit. We must mobilize within our church walls to begin reaching outside of them in hopes of finding the poor, the hurting, the brokenhearted. Trust me when I tell you that the single mother in your community who does not attend church is usually all three.

Of course, there will not be hundreds of single parents in every congregation. The size and location of your church will determine the size of the single moms ministry required to meet the needs of the single moms in your community. If we begin to actively seek out and draw in the millions of single parents who are outside our church walls, however, we will begin growing our churches, cultivating fellowship, and creating opportunities for hurting people to encounter the compassion that is the saving grace of Christ.

Let's explore God's call to action.

### Deuteronomy 14:29

"Give it to the Levites, who will receive no allotment of land among you, as well as to the foreigners living among you, the orphans, and the widows in your towns, so they can eat and be satisfied. Then the Lord your God will bless you in all your work."

### Isaiah 1:17

"Learn to do good. Seek justice. Help the oppressed. Defend the cause of orphans. Fight for the rights of widows."

### James 1:27

"Pure and genuine religion in the sight of God the Father means caring for orphans and widows in their distress ..."

### 1 Samuel 2:8

"He lifts the poor from the dust and the needy from the garbage dump."

### Psalm 82:3

"Give justice to the poor and orphan; uphold the rights of the oppressed and destitute."

### Luke 3:11

"John replied, 'If you have two shirts, give one to the poor. If you have food, share it with those that are hungry.'"

I'll stop right there, for now. There are countless scripture passages throughout the Old and New Testaments that instruct God's people to be active in serving the less fortunate, the poor, the hurting, the marginalized of the world. This is the single mom! I do not think most Christians would argue that point. It is quite exciting to see that the church in our day is beginning to grasp the concept of serving on a broader scale. But the fact remains that fewer than 1 in 100 churches in the United States have a single- parent ministry. We have soup kitchens, clothing programs, and widows' ministries, but a single mom's ministry? It is still, in many cases, a foreign concept.

## A "new" ministry need for a changed world

To understand why, we really must delve into our changing times. Forty years ago, there was little need for such a ministry. Of course, 40 years ago there was no such thing as profanity on network television; 30, 20, even 10 ten years ago, there was not nearly as much profanity, partial nudity, or sexual promiscuity as there is on prime-time network TV today. I can remember as an adolescent being embarrassed if there was even kissing on television, especially in front of my parents, much less anything more risqué than that! It is hard to find a channel (of the hundreds avail- able) that does not broadcast questionable material—*at least* when it comes to morality. And that's just the programming in the middle of the day!

No matter where we turn—to the Internet, television, radio, books, magazines, or the other countless forms of media, we are inundated with raw sexual content, glorified impurity, and loose morality. News programs feature the stories. Movies glorify them. Pop artists sing about them. We are suffering from an obvious desensitization to all things impure and immoral. Divorces are now the norm. In fact, in many circles, the moral "high road," the one of the highest biblical standard, is dismissed as intolerant and close-minded.

*How can this be?* When asked, approximately 78% of Americans identify themselves as Christian. So where are all the Christians when it comes to standing up for the biblical principles of our day and time? Why have we stood by and allowed the moral deterioration of our country so that "anything goes"?

A few years ago I was invited to go speak at a venue where

approximately 90% of the audience would be unwed, unchurched single mothers. I prayed about what the topic should be. I soon felt the burden to speak on sexual purity. Well, as you can probably imagine, I was extremely excited to cover that topic. (Sigh….) I was nervous, but I committed to study on the topic and gather statistics. I prayed and fasted.

I began to feel a strong pull in my heart to address some of the causes of sexual impurity. Of course, there is our sinful nature to contend with. But what about the barrage that assaults us from every media outlet? What about the television programming and music that we pour into our spirit? I decided to print the lyrics of some popular songs to read during my message to really drive the point home. I gasped when I pulled up the lyrics of one of the most popular songs of the year on the Internet. The lyrics were so sexually explicit that I could not even read them in a church setting! That confirmed in my mind once and for all that what we feed our spirits will surely come out. The music we pour in, the movies we view, that which we allow our children to hear, most certainly affects our actions.

The point is: Just as a drug addict does not wake up one morning craving crack cocaine, having never before sampled other illegal substances, neither do we wake up one day sexually impure. We don't just jump into sexual sin with both feet. Rather, it is a gradual descent into a life that is spiraling out of control. The same is true of what is happening in our country.

## A single mom in Bible times: Hagar

Think about Hagar in the Old Testament. Do you know her story? Many of us are familiar with Abraham and Sarah's wonderful story of God's faithfulness to fulfill his promises. And for many of us, that is where the story ends. But when we explore the story in its entirety, we see that another family is also involved.

In Gene- sis 16:1–6, we find that Hagar, the Egyptian "handmade" (or servant) of Sarah, was pregnant with Abraham's child. This was due mainly to Sarah's impatience with God's timing.

Later, after Sarah had borne to Abraham the son of God's promise, Isaac, we find that Sarah and Hagar quarreled and Hagar left the Hebrews with her son (by Abraham), Ishmael (Genesis 21:1- 21). Hagar went on to raise her son alone—as a single mom—in the wilderness. She cried out to God. She was alone and full of fear. *How would she provide for him? Would her son die? How would she feed and clothe him? Would her son grow up properly without a father?* I even wonder if Hagar was angry. She may have wondered: "Why can't Abraham raise Ishmael the same way he is raising his other son, Isaac?!" I am sure that she worried about and fretted over all of these things.

To be honest, I had never given much thought to Hagar and Ishmael. And I definitely had never fully comprehended the ramifications of being an unwed single mom in Bible times. Most accounts of the story of Abraham and Sarah focus on the great miracle of God's promise fulfilled in Isaac. Hagar was mentioned only for her role as a member of the supporting cast. As I delved deeper into the story, however, I came to believe that God has much to teach us about Hagar. The Bible later says that God heard Hagar's cry and made her son father of many nations (Genesis 21:17–20). Ishmael was actually conceived in sin and disobedience. He was ultimately fatherless. But God made him father over many descendants. Why do you think that Hagar and Ishmael are so crucial to Abraham's story?

## God's plans are always full of hope

Since the beginning of time, God has used the hopeless to bring hope, the impossible to make possible. Just because we have seen a deterioration in the moral fiber of our country does not give us Christians license to retreat—pack it in and wait on Heaven. In fact, it should motivate us to persevere and fight the good fight. It is important that we understand that, no matter what circumstances led to the conception of a child, we do not know of God's future plan. This is not just about the single mothers; we are also looking at the futures of their children.

How do we know that God has not called one of these children to be a future president of the United States? Or the next Billy Graham? The next Mother Teresa? We know that all life is precious. We know that "all things work for the good of those who love the Lord and are called according to his purpose" (Romans 8:28). We also know that "all have sinned" (Romans 3:23). With that said, we want to be careful that we are not avoiding launching a single moms ministry in our churches out of fear that doing so would somehow be supporting or condoning sexual sin. As ludicrous as that may sound, I have actually heard that argument!

Recently a gentleman approached me (in reference to a single mother's ministry) and said, "Why is it that you feel that it is the church's responsibility to teach the single mother? This message starts at home. It is the father's responsibility. It is the parents' responsibility."

Okay, so let's camp out on this argument for a moment. There is plenty of biblical teaching on parents' responsibility for teaching and raising their children in a God-honoring fashion. Agreed. The father is also the God-ordained head of the household and should provide wise counsel and instruction for his children. Agreed. But what the gentleman's line of thinking failed to answer were the prevailing questions: "What do we do with all the single mothers who in our country now? What about all the fatherless homes? Does this in some way insinuate that all single-parent homes were somehow a punishment for sin?!"

Let me respond. First of all, as we have already discussed, the Bible is quite clear about our obligation to help the poor, the widows, and the fatherless. That instruction alone is reason enough for us to get active in ministering to these women. But let me take it a step further. I agree that parental involvement, teaching abstinence, and emphasizing the importance of protecting the holy union of matrimony are all important steps in preventing unwed pregnancy and divorce.

But that does not address the millions of single parents in our country right now. And what about the virgin who married just after high school and has served the Lord all the days of her life, only to have her husband come home one day and announce that he is leaving her and wants a divorce? She is now a divorced, single mom, who has done nothing to deserve it. Where does she go for care and encouragement? If the "it's not the church's responsibility" line of thinking held true and all resources and care are the responsibility of the family, then the answer would be "nowhere." She would simply drown in the sea of overwhelming responsibility and have to fend for herself and her children alone. Is that "am I sister's keeper?" response true to the graceful good news of Jesus Christ?

We are currently seeing generations of single parents raising new generations of single parents. We are in a crisis. We cannot cite one statistic that supports an argument that a single-parent home is the most effective place to raise a child. Quite the contrary. We have already cited dozens of statistics that suggest just the opposite. But how does a single parent ministry change any of this?

What we have seen in our own single moms ministry (one of the largest in the nation) and in many others around the country is that single mothers who have regular meetings with a local support network are more willing to share about those things with which they are burdened. Research shows that being able to talk about their issues decreases the risk of abuse within their homes.

We have also found that single mothers are more open to coming into a church environment when they are surrounded by other single moms who are in a similar situation. They do not feel judged or embarrassed. They are not "the only ones."

Because they share this common bond, they are more open to asking for help with parenting and finances. They can get biblical advice on how to handle life's challenges. They learn and grow in the Lord. When the single moms ministry is developed fully, we see these women growing in effective parenting skills, wisdom in financial matters, emotional stability, and spiritual maturity. And what is most encouraging is that many of these moms, who were not actively attending church prior to the single moms ministries, transition into active membership in their new church homes. Thus, not only is this ministry a viable means of reaching outside the church walls, but it has also been proven to grow the church congregation.

CHAPTER **4**

# FEAR

*Let perfect love cast out fear…*

T he fear some churches have that launching a single moth- er's ministry in some way condones (or even *encourages)* divorce or sexual immorality or glamorizes the lifestyle is completely unfounded. Thankfully, this fear is not widespread, and many churches are beginning to see the need. But if you are part of one of the churches still concerned, consider this.

"Get rid of all bitterness, rage, anger, harsh words, and slander, as well as all types of evil behavior." (Ephesians 4:31 NLT)

If we can't do single moms ministry because it encourages single-parenthood, then by the same logic that would mean that we have to omit liars, back-stabbers, and slanderers from our men's Bible studies, right? Would we not also have to tell gossipers that they could not come to our ladies' events? They are sinners, right? This is the flip-side of what people are saying when they proclaim, "I do not go to church because there are too many hypocrites there."

Yet, isn't it interesting how those same people don't let the "hypocrites" keep them from attending a favorite sporting event or going to the grocery store?

Fear within the church is only part of the problem, though. I have spoken to many frustrated leaders who do, in fact, have single mom ministries in their churches, but they are stagnant and not growing. They feel that, although they have done everything they can to make the environment safe for the moms to come, there is little commitment from the single mom and very little growth. This frustration often stems from our lack of understanding of the single mom's situation. In chapter 8 we will discuss ways to grow your ministry in more detail, but for now let me take you into the single mom's world.

## The world of the single mom

She is scared and alone. A million thoughts are running through her mind, depending on her story. She is surrounded by loving couples who are still together, and everyone's life seems perfect compared to her own. She begins to question everything.

"How am I a single mother? I have served the Lord all my life! Why has my husband left me? Am I being punished?"

"Will my son grow up to be successful with no father in his life?"

"I am damaged goods. I have had multiple sexual partners and now I have a kid. No one will ever want me, especially a good, Christian man."

"How could God allow this to happen to me?"

"How will we ever make it financially?"

"I am never going to church again. That church has not been there for me! If they cared, they would have counseled my husband about leaving his wife, before he ran off with another woman. Now he and his new girlfriend go to church there. How could the church let them attend?"

"I never expected to get pregnant. One night. And now… everyone knows what I have been doing. I am an embarrassment to my family and to everyone around me. What am I going to do now?"

Dozens, probably hundreds, of other thoughts just like these are swarming through the mind of a new single mom.

It is true that when a tragedy erupts in our lives many of us give church a try. Even someone who has not been to church in months or years will somehow make her way back to church, hoping for some type of emotional relief. The same is true for the woman who experiences an unplanned pregnancy, unexpected death, or divorce. Many times, they will "give the church thing a try." What we do when they get here is key.

I have counseled hundreds of women through the years. Initially, my focus was on teen mothers and young, unwed mothers. As the ministry grew, I began to work with more and more divorced moms. Honestly, I was shocked at the amount of bitterness and anger that many of them carried. I mean, I knew my own journey of unplanned pregnancy, abuse, and poverty, but I had never gone through divorce. In some ways, I think that subconsciously I had deemed that the "easier" of the single-parenting journeys.

The bitterness and anger in my own life was largely from abuse and the failure of my children's father to support them. But I quickly learned that the divorced mom has that same bitterness. There is not an "easier" journey for single moms—divorced, widowed, or unplanned. Even long-time Christian women go through different phases of the divorce process, and most will eventually find themselves in the midst of bitterness and anger.

Through the years, I have heard many divorcing women spew venom at the church, their pastors, family members, friends, and their ex-husbands. I am not saying that none of that anger is founded. But I was surprised to learn how widespread the anger was towards the church. In some ways that almost seemed to be the deepest of hurts. Some may see this whole book as an attack on the church and a way for me to list everything the church is doing wrong. Not at all. I honor the church. Jesus loved the church and died for it. I am thankful to my own church family for all they have done through the years and what a comforting place my church has been in my life. Millions of people around the world would say the same of their own churches. But … I do understand now how a divorcing woman can, even if only for a season, go through this anger.

For a married woman who has attended church with her husband and children for many years, been a faithful tither, and by most accounts "done everything right," the devastation of a failed marriage can be almost too much to bear. There is the immediate question, "Why God? How could you have allowed this to hap- pen?!" She can begin to question her whole walk with the Lord or Christianity, in general. She replays every little thing she could have possibly done differently. She aches. Maybe she and her husband tried counseling. Maybe her husband began to drift away from the church.

## Be sensitive to her fear and pain

She then moves on to other questions. "Didn't the church see that we were hurting? Why didn't they do more? Why didn't the pastor come visit us? Why didn't the Bible study leader reach out more?" Just as the church is usually the place that many people run to for emotional comfort in times of crisis, it is often the first place people blame for the very crisis.

The first time I ever received a phone message peppered with profanity from a single mom I was ministering to, I was crushed. I had been working with the single mom for months, and one day, out of the blue, she left me a very detailed, profanity-laced phone message about how I did not really care about her and that I had not done enough to help her. I was in utter disbelief. Boy, was I naïve! It is sad to say that through the years I have had a few calls of that type and the occasional *difficult* email. What I once took so personally I now see as a cry for help. The call has absolutely nothing to do with me personally. I just happened to be the one who was in the line of fire. Hurting people sometimes hurt others. The same is true of the church and/or ministry leadership. Many times, there is nothing you could have done differently. You are simply the first one in their line of fire. They will say to you what they really want to say to their ex-spouse, childhood abuser, or any number of other relationships represented in their lives.

I am not excusing the behavior, but as a recipient of God's amazing grace in my own life—over and over and over again—I choose to forgive a hurting woman who happens to say the wrong thing in the midst of her pain. As the body of Christ, let's be certain that we are sensitive to the fear and pain that these women are feeling and that we guard our own hearts against offense about what may be said in a time of anger. Understand that our goal is to love each other through crisis, rather than judge the reason why it occurred.

CHAPTER 5

# THE HURT: THE STORY BEHIND THE FACE

*In their own words…*

As we launched our national campaign to assist churches in starting a single moms ministry, the letters began to pour in. In this chapter I would like to introduce you to some of my new friends who have allowed me to use their stories. With permission, each woman's story has been edited only slightly and with the intention of preserving and conveying its true emotion and authenticity. I wanted to take you on a journey through the lives of many across the country so that you can feel the hurt and see the pain. You will discover that the single-mom crisis is no respecter of persons. It transcends all demographics and occurs for women in all age groups, racial and ethnic profiles, educational backgrounds, religious denominations, and socio-economic statuses.

## Rowesha's story

I am a 30-year-old single mother of one who lives in Dallas, Texas. I have been a single mother since my daughter's birth two years ago. I thought I could just settle and still be happy with my child's father. (Boy, was I wrong!) We never married, and our relationship has been tumultuous, to say the least. Being a single mother is the hardest thing I have ever done. I never expected to be here. I graduated college, married my college sweetheart, and pictured everything perfect.

It was not long before he began to abuse me, and the marriage ended. It was the loneliest time of my life. I met a new guy, fell in love, and before I knew it, I found myself pregnant. Children change everything. Not only am I alone, but raising my daughter seems to be my sole responsibility. I am exhausted—mentally, financially, and emotionally. As a first-time mother who is also single, I feel trapped. I feel like I am suffocating. I have no time to myself and wonder if I will always be alone.

I was raised in church but fell away when I got older. I now find myself attending again. Church offers an encouraging word, but the battles come daily. I do not have a support group at church, and although I attend weekly, I still have not found a church to call "home." Honestly, if it weren't for a group of older women on my job, I do not think I could make it.

## Josie's story

I am a 24-year-old single mother who lives in Henderson, Nevada. I have a two-year-old daughter who is the light of my life. My family never attended church when I was growing up. I did, however, occasionally visit local churches with friends. I was always searching for something, but no church ever held my interest for very long. At one point, I even seriously considered converting to Judaism. In my late

teens and early college years, I was doing anything and everything that was exciting in the moment with no care about consequences. My life was literally sex, drugs, and rock 'n' roll. I ended up pregnant at 21. My daughter's father quickly ducked out of the picture. I started attending church because I realized that I did not have much moral guidance growing up and did not want the same for my own daughter.

No one ever told me that you should wait until marriage to have sex or that I did not need to sleep with men to make them love me. I definitely did not believe the whole "Jesus thing." A friend of mine was attending a local church and invited me. Everyone there was nice and friendly. About a month later, a pastor was preaching on forgiveness. I realized that I was still harboring great anger towards my child's father. A few moments later, I found myself in the midst of a prayer asking God to forgive my sins and to help me forgive others.

It was the best decision I ever made. Through the church, I have found hope and freedom. My church offers a single moms program that has allowed me to actively serve with them and develop friendships. Life is funny. When I found out I was pregnant, I thought my life was over. Little did I know that the Lord was using that moment to save me.

## Haley's story

I became a single mom at 23. I was raised in Detroit, Michigan. I was in church when I was younger but had slipped away. After my daughter was born, I knew I had to go back. I had to turn my life around. I wanted my daughter to know Christ in the way that I had known him … in the way that I needed to know him again.

I finally mustered the courage to attend a service at a small church in my hometown. I quickly realized there was no one there like me—no single moms. As I walked into the building Sunday after Sunday, I thought I would instantly feel a burden lifted, like I was coming home.

Instead, I had a constant feeling of being an outsider. I felt like everyone else who sinned could hide it, but not me. I walked around with the evidence of my sin all the time. It felt like a scarlet letter was sewn on my shirt. I was never ashamed of my daughter, but I was very ashamed of what everyone knew I had done to get her.

It was not what the church did to me, but rather what they did *not* do. They did not try to get to know me. I was not invited to any fellowships. There seemed to be no group at church where I belonged or where I fit in. I know now that some of it was my own guilt because I had a hard time forgiving myself. I needed someone to reach out to me. I wanted someone to let me know that it was okay for me to be part of the church, despite what I had done. I needed to feel like I was forgiven, not only by God and myself, but by my church. I never found it there.

## Sharon's story

I am a 27-year-old single mother of twin boys who are now six. I have legally been a single mother for about four years, but I have raised my children alone for most of the six years. I come from a middle-class Catholic family that went to church every Sunday. I was confirmed Catholic at 17 but always struggled in really connecting to God. My childhood was pleasant. I was an honor-roll student who was involved in dancing and various clubs at school. By most accounts I was a typical all-American teen girl.

My great-grandfather abused both my great-grandmother and my grandmother both emotionally and physically. I later learned that my mother became pregnant with me when she was only 15 years old. These are things that my family considers awkward and talking about them is frowned upon.

I found myself pregnant at 21 with my serious boyfriend. We immediately moved in together and were married soon thereafter. He is a man whom most would consider financially successful. After we married, something seemed to switch in him. He became extremely neglectful of me. He also became verbally, physically, and emotionally abusive. He never had to be directly forceful with sex, but I always knew that it was not really an option. He drank heavily and began using drugs. He began cheating on me regularly. After confessing that he had been unfaithful to me four times, he admitted to me that he had been abused by numerous men in his life and that he was a sex addict. He refused to get help and I later divorced him.

As my life was spiraling out of control, I began to seek out Jesus. I had asked for salvation in 10th grade but never truly understood what that meant. I went through a period of depression, loneliness, and a hundred other emotions. But, thank God, I was set free from my past and am learning to lean on him more each day. Although I sometimes still struggle with "religion," I know that through my hurt and pain I found Jesus.

## Barbara's story

I am a 40-year-old mother of two—a four-year old girl and a six-year-old boy. I was born and raised in Round Rock, Texas. I was raised in a good Christian home with parents who loved me. My parents had lost their 13-year-old child in an accident, so they were extremely overprotective of me.

I can remember accepting Christ as my Savior, just like it was yesterday. I walked to the front of the church to announce my decision. I had no direction after that. I thought I was fine—nothing else to do with this Christian walk.

When I got older, I wanted freedom from my parents' restrictions and I sought it through a cool boyfriend who was a rock 'n' roll drummer. He was a rebel, and I was the proverbial "good girl" who simply wanted to be popular. I almost immediately thought this guy was bad for me and even broke up with him, but I found it hard to stay away. After about a year of dating, my mother felt sorry for him (because his father was dead and his mother was an alcoholic) and decided to help take care of him.

By our senior year in high school, my mother regularly defended him, even when he mistreated me or cheated on me, citing that he was only doing because of his tragic upbringing. She made excuses for him and supported him, sometimes even more than she supported me. I came to a point, even knowing in my heart that he was not good for me, when I could not let go of him. I would not allow myself to accept the reality of being without him.

One week before our wedding, he slapped me across the face and threw my clothes out. I wanted to cancel the wedding, but at 23, I was simply too scared to take such a big step. Six years into our rocky marriage, I began to really desire a baby. Instead of a baby, my husband desired a new career and joined a band. He began playing in local bars. Things got progressively worse. He began having affairs, two of which were long-term, simultaneous affairs. I was devastated.

A friend had been inviting me back to church, and two days before my 30th birthday, I went. My life was at the lowest of lows. I was broken. My visit to the local church was different. This church was unlike any I had gone to before. I felt a little awkward, but I needed some peace in my life. I began listening to Christian music and attending church faithfully. The whole time my husband continued to have an affair, but God brought me to 1 Corinthians 7:13–15. I clung to that scripture for the next year, in the darkest of times.

My husband continued his affair and even began remodeling a room in his mother's home so that he could move in there. I was so sick of this limbo stage that I was in. I prayed and prayed. Finally, in August 2002, my husband went to church with me and went to the altar for prayer. I was elated! It finally happened! We were on the road to recovery!

Two years later, I gave birth to my first child and, a little later, to a second. Things seemed to be going perfectly … until my husband was asked to play in a church band at a new church. He developed some friendships and connections through the church band and almost instantly began playing in local bars again. My husband eventually became addicted to crack cocaine. Our lives spiraled out of control, yet again.

My husband left me, moved in with another woman, and has struggled with a cocaine addiction for years now. He hardly ever sees his two young children. It has been hard to walk out this journey in my life. I have been embarrassed by the divorce, angry at the church, and even angry at God at times. But through it all, I am thankful that I have had a relationship with Christ to help me through it and the support of my local single moms group.

## Angela's story

I am a 58-year old mother of four from Nebraska. I came from a strict Christian home and married straight out of high school. I tried to do everything right for my husband. He was controlling and manipulative. Although we attended church every Sunday, behind closed doors he was beating me. My husband was a successful businessman who was influential in the community. Every single day, I felt as though I was slowly dying. Twenty years and four children later, I was still that sad, lonely woman who never felt confident enough to tell anyone what I was going through. I suffered through church. I wanted to disappear.

In addition to the abuse, my husband had affairs and was addicted to pornography. I felt worthless. After 21 years of marriage, my husband came home from work one day and announced that he was in love with another woman and thus would be leaving the family. He also told me that I was no longer welcome at our church because he and his mistress would marry and attend that church.

I had never worked outside the home. How would I support myself and the kids? I lost my life. What had I done to deserve this? I lost my church. I had nothing. How would I ever survive? That was four years ago. Since then, the struggles I have gone through financially and emotionally are almost unimaginable for most. But I made it. It is only just now that I have wanted to reconnect to church. I have tried out a few churches but have not yet found one to call home. I don't even know where to start.

## Helena's story

I am 19 years old. I have three children. Although we have moved around, I am now living in Jacksonville, Florida. I live with my mom. My dad has never been around, because he has been in and out of jail most of my life. My mom has used drugs most of my life. She always has a "boyfriend." I do not even remember how old I was when her boyfriends began to touch me. The only time I ever told her about it she beat me up. Maybe she needs them more than she needs me.

I am not dumb, as some people may think. I was always on honor roll in school until I had to drop out because there was no one to watch my babies while I went. My life is not where I wanted it to be, but I guess no one's is. I am surprised I am here. I need help.

## Mary's story

Jesus? Who is he? I know you do not want me to believe there is a God! Because if there was, then he surely would not let me live the way I have lived. He would not let my kids go hungry. He would not let me go hungry. The church folks? They do not care. They just sit on their high-horse and tell the rest of us how to live! I don't need 'em.

## Jenn's Story

I am 16 years old. When I was a little kid, I used to sing in the children's choir at church. All my friends and I go to church every Sunday. We all sit together. My parents are strict, but I love them. I have had a good life. But right now, I feel like just dying. I just found out that I am pregnant. I have not told anyone. I have been hiding it for a few weeks and am scared to death. I have been in church all my life. I did not mean for this to happen. My boyfriend is part of our church youth group. I love him and know that he loves me, but he's scared, too. We are only in 11th grade.

One night. One mistake.

This is so stupid. I am a good girl. I am a straight-A student. I made one bad choice and am going to pay for this forever. My parents are going to kill me. They are going to be so ashamed of me. I am embarrassed. No one is going to understand. I want to crawl under my bed and never come out. Make this go away! I don't feel like I belong anywhere. I cannot even think about God. I know he must hate me. I hate myself. Will you please help me tell my mom?


These are only a handful of the hundreds of stories that pour into our email each year. I love it that some of the women have found a church home and are reaching out to find out more about the ministry we run. Sadly, however, many of the emails I get are cries for help from the lost and hurting who dare not enter the local church. Each time that I am certain I have heard the worst story, the most severe abuse, the most dire of circumstances, I meet a new woman—a new pain.

Sometimes the simplest ministry is just a compassionate heart. I want to share one last story with you, the story of a young woman who came to our single moms ministry here in Baton Rouge, Louisiana. Meet Callie….

## Callie's Story

As the leader of the single mother's ministry at our local church, I often get phone calls from single moms who have been referred to me or the names of single moms whom I need to follow up with. One Sunday afternoon, I began placing my regular phone calls and stumbled upon a young lady named Callie. I called to introduce myself.

"Hi, Callie. My name is Jennifer Maggio. I run the single moms program at our local church. I was given your information because you attended one of our weekend services. I wanted to tell you all about what we do for single moms."

"Ummmm…. I've never attended a service there," Callie told me. "I came to the church the other day for food."

"Oh, I'm sorry. I must have misunderstood, but it's no problem at all. I am glad we were able to help you. I wanted to talk to you about—"

"Before you get started with your whole little speech," Callie interrupted, "I had better interrupt you. If you knew everything about me, you probably would not even be talking with me!"

As the conversation went on, Callie explained to me that she was a 20-year-old single mom of a 4-year-old little boy and was currently expecting a second baby. She was originally from Michigan but relocated to the south with her boyfriend. She never actively attended church and was not even sure there was a God. In fact, she was a self-proclaimed witch and was certain that that very statement would make me hang up on her!

My response? "Girl, you just come to our single moms group and we will get you in a safe place where we can help you!"

(I somehow knew that spewing endless Bible verses to her and attempting to convince her of God's existence, much less presence, would be to no avail. Right now, in this moment, Callie did not need a "hellfire and brimstone" sermon. She needed a friend.) "Well … ummmm … I may come to your little meeting. I'm not sure. *If* I do, then there is something you should know. I wear something everywhere I go and if you make me take it off, I will not come to your group!"

"Awww, honey, you just come on in with whatever you have on," I replied in my friendliest Southern accent. "We are extremely casual and we just want *you* there."

I ended the conversation and honestly assumed I would never hear from her again. To my great surprise, the following weekend, Callie showed up at our single moms group. I could not believe it. I instantly knew it was her because around her neck I saw the item she vowed that she would never remove—it was a necklace with an upside down cross attached to it. (For those of you who are unfamiliar with this symbol, the upside cross is often used to symbolize mockery of Jesus Christ and is often seen in the occult.) We welcomed her in, hugged her, and ushered her up to the front row as we began the evening's message.

Callie did not say much after that first meeting. Over the next several months, however, Callie became one of our most faithful attenders. As we began to learn more about Callie, we discovered that she was currently living in a small travel trailer that was decrepit and almost falling down. The only way she could heat food was on one small burner—the same burner she used to heat the trailer. She worked full-time as a waitress at a local diner and lived with her fiancé. She explained that her fiancé was the high priest of the cult that she was forced into. Her 4-year-old had been removed from her home due to her occult activity and drug use.

As a former abuse victim, she was desperate for someone to love her, and when her now fiancé came along, she grasped at the hopes of a relationship. What she later found was not a healthy relation- ship with a man who would take care of her, but rather an extremely abusive, manipulative man who forced her into the occult and later into prostitution. The baby she was now carrying was not her fiancé's child but rather the result of a prostitution encounter.

We worked with her for months, providing her love, resources, and friendship. After a meeting one night, she asked to speak with me. We stepped into a corner down the hall and she said, "I have something to tell you. Tonight is my last night in town. I have a ride waiting in the parking lot who has agreed to drive me back to my family in Michigan. I have already talked to them. They want me home and I am leaving this life behind. I want you to know how much this group has meant to me."

She stopped and pulled something from her purse. It was a brand-new Bible that we had given her weeks earlier. "Jennifer," she continued, "this is the first Bible I have ever owned. This is the first time I have ever felt comfortable in church. Because of this group, I want something different in my life. My mom has already contacted our local pastor, and we are going to start church right away."

We hugged and cried. It confirmed for me every reason why I do what I do. I never heard from Callie again. I do not know if she went on to change her life and live a successful God-honoring life. Perhaps I never will. But what I do know is that we planted a seed with a young girl who would never have attended church had it not been for Healing Place Church Single Moms Ministry.

There are thousands of "Callies" in our neighborhoods and com- munities. They are waiting for someone to grab them by the hand and show them the hope that is Jesus Christ.

*They are waiting for you….*

CHAPTER 6

# WHERE DO YOU FIND HER?

*How to reach her and draw her in...*

As we have already discussed, the broken are often coming to our churches to give them "a test drive," to find relief, but if there is not a miraculous healing in that first few visits, many fall away. This fact alone puts a great deal of pressure on the church. I would propose that single moms are visiting or attending almost every one of our churches across the country at some point or another.

Perhaps she is the one who sits in the back, quietly. Maybe she is the one who attends on Sundays but avoids conversations or additional Bible studies at all costs. If there is a battle internally about whether or not they belong in the church, then there is most certainly an all-out war when they arrive! Any insecurity, hurt, bitterness, or disappointment can and will resurface. It is Satan's oldest and most predictable trick.

If we are increasingly aware of the single moms in our church and are prepared to help them handle their hurt, pain, and offense, then we are infinitely better-prepared to reach not only her but all the single moms she represents.

*How do we do that? What do we say?*

I spoke recently to a group of single moms at an engagement on "Beauty: From the Inside Out." The church hosted a "Night of Beauty" for single moms to come and enjoy free makeovers, hand treatments, spa gift certificates, and free bottles of designer perfume. It was intricate and lovely. The room was abuzz with excitement over the giveaways. When everyone was seated I began to share. The following is a portion of what I said.

> Every woman in this room is breathtakingly beautiful. You take your Father's breath away. Don't believe me?

> Read Genesis 2:21–23: "And the Lord God cast a deep slumber on the human (Adam), and he slept. He took one of Adam's ribs and closed over the flesh where it had been, and the Lord God built the rib He had taken from the human into a woman and He brought her to the human."

> Isn't it amazing that God chose to create us last? It was not an afterthought, but rather the "piece de resistance." God made each of us with intention, not as an accident, but in His perfect image. He intended for you to have the hair you do, the shape you do, and the physical features you do. It was not by accident that you are not a size 0. Just because *Elle* magazine says you need to be 100 pounds with long blond hair does not make it so. Single moms, for far too long, we have been putting lipstick on a wound that it could not possibly heal.

> We focus on the outer beauty, which most of us feel we will never measure up to, rather than concentrating on those things that make us radiant from the inside out. We feel that our physical beauty is easier to control than the "ugly" within us. We long to be desired, just as God created us to be, and

because most of us have been abandoned or rejected, we shut down that inner vulnerable place that is the very essence of a woman. We hide from it.

It is easier to change hair color than it is to change the root of bitterness that we have allowed to grow from the divorce or failed relationship. It is easier to purchase a new perfume than it is to cleanse the stench of offense that others can smell from a mile away.

Single mothers, do you want to know the one thing that will empower your parenting skills and equip you to press forward? Understand who you are in Christ! Do not live in past sin, allowing the shame and embarrassment to consume you. Stand on God's word that says that nothing separates us from his love. Allow the beauty that is the Holy Spirit living on the inside of you to shine through—the joy that is found in him, the peace that is most assuredly only found in him! Stop living as the victim but claim your *victory*."

As you can imagine, the room did not erupt with applause. The sting of truth resonated with many of the women present, and I needed to let them digest it. The preceding is simply one example of the types of things that a single mom really needs to hear. The manner in which we deliver the truth, however, is key. I am able to share truth with a single mom in a way that she will most often be able to receive because I am a former single mom. I don't have to imagine what it is like and what she is feeling and the challenges she is facing. I *know* because I have been there and experienced it all firsthand. I have immediate credibility. I am "one of them." I understand.

This enables single moms to open up and share more freely with me. They sense no judgment from me. A single mom desperately needs to know that there are others like her. She is not alone in her predicament. We all want to develop relationships with those who understand. We long to know that we are not the only ones out there in a particular situation.

## She needs to know that you understand

But as she is trying out new churches, the single mom also wants to know that the church understands her. You, the pastor. You, the elder. You, the married woman who has never been divorced. You, the Sunday School teacher. You, the neighbor seated on the pew next to her. She wants to know that you understand—that you care enough to try to understand—even if you have never experienced it yourself. She needs to know that your compassion in Christ allows you to understand her. She needs to know that she belongs there on the pew next to you. She needs to know that when the time is right, she will receive truth about her situation and not simply be ignored altogether.

Notice here that I said, "when the time is right." An initial conversation in the church pew does not need to lead into a 10-minute sermonette about her bitterness, her anger, and her sin. The Holy Spirit is perfect in delivering opportunities to share at the appropriate time. The initial contact is an opportunity for you to be kind, friendly, caring, and helpful in sharing all the ways this single mom can get involved in your church.

## How to find the single moms in your community

You may be thinking "That is fine advice when I have a single mom sitting right next to me in church, but how do we find the ones who are beyond our doors?" There are many ways to find the single mom. I will highlight only a few:

- Create fliers to advertise your Sunday services and Single Moms Ministry. Pass them out at local apartment complexes and housing projects.
- Distribute fliers at daycare centers. (Almost 70% of children in daycare centers come from single-parent homes.)
- Create a link from your church Web site highlighting what you are doing for single moms. In my research, I have found that many of the churches who already offer single mom ministries merely mention it on the church calendar but do not provide a detailed link to outline what a new single mom can expect.
- Open up social media pages for single moms, such as Face-book and Twitter.
- Have business cards printed and begin to pass them out freely. I have found that local grocery stores are ideal. As I am doing my own weekly shopping, the Lord has opened up many doors for me to introduce myself and inquire about whether or not a mom is single. Having a business card with me always helps.
- Plan community outreaches specifically for the single mom, such as free car care, free garage sales, family fun days, etc. There are a number of creative ways to minister to single moms in your community. For more ideas, visit www.thelifeofasinglemom.com.
- Leave business cards at nursery check-in on Sundays so that nursery providers can easily provide your information to visitors.
- Set up booths at local fairs.

- Advertise your event on Christian radio stations, such as K-LOVE. Public service announcements (PSAs) are a free serv- ice that many Christian networks offer.

- Ask to leave business cards at hospitals (for those who are giving birth and bringing home infants alone).

- Ask to leave business cards at local crisis pregnancy clinics.

- Leave fliers at doctors' offices and the community health centers.

These are just a few ways you can begin to publicize your single moms ministry. When you reach out actively to the community you communicate your desire to help the single mom and let them know what your ministry is doing for them. When we reach out in this way to bring in the unchurched we are fulfilling Christ's commission to go and make disciples. This is exactly what we, the church, want. We should never be content to let our churches become the local social club, designed to keep others out, while making ourselves feel better about who we are.

Church is that place of solace, that place of rest. We offer hope through Christ that the world cannot give. Our desire is to have people leave our services saying, "Wow, there is just something about that church. The people are so warm and friendly. They are so full of joy. What is it?" We want the unchurched to be drawn in by our openness to allow Christ to shine through us.

## Two situations to handle with care

### *Attending the group as a bargaining tool*

As our single moms ministry has grown, we have had two situations arise that are important to note. The first situation is in reference to women who attend our single moms program who are separated from their husbands. Be careful here. Our position is always—*always*—to hope and pray that there is a radical transformation within their marriages, that spouses are saved, and repentance occurs. Our hope is for the restoration of marriage. That is our constant prayer. And yes, we have seen God do the miraculous within marriages within our single moms ministry. Single moms who were temporarily separated have experienced a restoration of their marriage and they go on to serve in our church. It is a beautiful thing.

Communicate clearly, however, that single mom ministries are never to be used as a bargaining tool between spouses. For example, you should encourage a woman who is experiencing a difficult season in her marriage to attend marriage counseling, marriage enrichment classes, and marriage seminars with her husband. Our church offers other women's Bible studies whereby women can lock arms with her during this difficult time. Our single moms program is available in the unfortunate event that a woman finds herself separated, living alone, and parenting alone. Our single moms program is *never* to be used as an outlet for moms who want to dangle a carrot in front of their husbands, such as "Fine you do not want to come home on time. You do not want to spend time with me. Then, I will just go to single moms group!"

As a leader, if you are made aware of such a situation, lovingly direct the mother to God's word on marriage and stand with her in prayer for the restoration of her marriage, then direct her to another, more appropriate support group. Defer to your church leadership with any questions you have about this type of situation.

### Attending the group because "I feel like a single mom"
The second situation that has arisen can be summed up in the common statement of married women who say, "May I attend the single moms group? I am not a single mom, but I feel like one. I do everything pretty much by myself. My husband rarely helps."

This is a wonderful opportunity for us to be kind, loving, and compassionate with our sisters who are obviously going through a difficult season. Again, as mentioned above, our focus is on the restoration of marriage, the knowledge that our God can and will perform miracles, and on helping those women who are actually single mothers (in fact not just in feeling). We have several programs in our church to offer guidance to women in many different stations in life—including widows, singles, married women, special interest groups, etc. Be careful to exhibit kindness in this instance, but also protect the integrity and intimacy of the single moms program.

We will allow a non-single mom support person, such as a neighbor, mom, or friend, to attend with a new single mom for one or two meetings, just to allow her to acclimate to the single moms group and become comfortable. We want our moms to come in and be comfortable, and we understand that some single moms may be more nervous or shy than others. We do not allow such support person to attend beyond a couple of meetings.

These may seem like such insignificant details, but as our continued focus is to foster an environment where single moms feel supported and connected and can grow in their relationship with the Lord, we want to minimize distractions as much as possible. For instance, a single mom could find out that a married woman is in the group (even in just a supporting role) and perhaps that will be the only thing she will choose to focus on for the night. Thus, the distraction completely hinders her ability to share or be ministered to. Again, we are focused on removing obstacles.

We have arrived! How exciting! We are at the point of launching the program. We see the need. We see the single mom and have some strategies for reaching her, and we want to make a difference. So, let's get started.

CHAPTER 7

## SHE'S HERE...NOW WHAT?
## 8 STEPS TO EFFECTIVE MINISTRY

*Best practices, tips, and how-to's to get you started...*

N ow, you are convinced that this ministry is relevant to your world. How do you get started? What do you do? We have devised a plan of best practices, tips, and how-to's to get you started. I want to make it clear that this is *not* a legalistic, must-be-done-this-way plan. Rather, it is a culmination of years of experience as well as first-hand knowledge of how to effectively run a single moms program. No two ministry settings are exactly alike, so you may need to make some adjustments to suit the particular needs of your church or non-profit.

### Step 1: Pray and seek wise counsel through your church leadership

This may seem obvious but let me explain. I consider a single moms ministry to be "high-level" ministry. It is time-consuming and at times exhausting. Often the women who find themselves at the point of an unplanned pregnancy or a failed marriage are hurting, broken, and needy—if only for a season. This simple fact alone means that you, the potential leader, need to be under the covering of your church so that they can support this endeavor. You must submit to your pastors' leadership and wisdom. The first step is to be diligent in seeking support from the leadership of the church. Satan would like nothing more than for you to be out on a limb, trying to run this type of ministry alone, in hopes of seeing you fail under the weight and pressure of it all. You must be surrounded by people who will pray for you and with you and be willing to submit to their authority. This is God's design (Ephesians 4:11–12, Acts 14:23, 1 Peter 5:1–2).

Once you have prayed and know that God is calling you to launch a program within the church, set up a meeting with your pastors (or appropriate members of the leadership team). I suggest having a detailed plan with you to keep you on track. The ministry plan should include the following:

- ***Statement of need:*** Gather statistics on single moms to raise awareness of what the single moms issues are and the effects on the church. (Feel free to use any statistics from this book.)

- ***Plan to address the need:*** Write out why you want to launch the ministry and some suggestions on how you see it functioning and how you could help. Your leadership team will appreciate the effort and prayer you have put forth, as well as diligence and planning.

Be open to suggestions and not easily offended. Again, this is such a special ministry, and one I believe is truly from the heart of God, so do not be surprised when something is said that could potentially hurt or offend you. Recognize it for what it is—a plan by the enemy to discourage you—and pray through it.

Just a personal note here. I struggled significantly with this step in the beginning, which is why I am lovingly explaining it to you.

Once God laid the single moms ministry on my heart and I submitted and resolved to actually do it (after God nudged me patiently for more than a year and I failed at convincing Him that He had chosen the wrong girl!), I was no-holds-barred. I wanted the ministry to start immediately. I thought it should be top priority on everyone's things-to-do list. And if it was not everyone's top priority, I was ready to go to war. There was such spiritual immaturity there on my part. I was simply so excited about the potential of reaching single moms that I often overstepped my authority in rushing decisions and the like. Understand that God has placed your church leadership team in authority, and we all have a role to play (Romans 12:6–11).

## Step 2: Recognize the top four areas where single moms can be served best

1. **Financial instruction**—In light of the recent economic turmoil across the globe, it is impossible for the local church to meet every financial need. When considering launching a single moms ministry, there could be concern that a single moms ministry will generate even more financial needs. Although sometimes we do provide financial assistance through our church, more often we provide financial counseling and resource lists.

   Financial instruction is a basic way to show single-parent house- holds (and all other Christian households) how to manage their money effectively and be good stewards. Financial difficulties often lead single moms to the church for assistance, which is a great way to get them connected to your single moms ministry. We suggest using Biblical principles to tackle such topics as how to budget and how to rectify a poor credit history. We recommend Dave Ramsey's *Financial Peace University* course. We also provide single moms with a list that details both local and national ministries that provide financial resources, such as assistance with utility bill payments, rent, etc. We update it frequently and have it available at the registration table at every meeting.

So, no matter what topic we are discussing for the night's meeting, the participants all know that they may obtain a list of financial resources at any time. The following Web site is a great place to begin building a resource list for your area:

www.thelifeofasinglemom.com

2. **Parenting advice**—Parenting advice is certainly one of the most obvious ways we can serve single-parent families. As we have discussed above, single-parent households have children who are more likely to go to prison, drop out of high school, commit suicide, and be abused. Intentional parenting is effective parenting. Because there is not a second opinion in the home, parenting alone can be especially difficult. Be certain that you are providing practical strategies that moms can implement immediately. Nothing is more frustrating to an already overwhelmed single mom than being taught detailed, time-consuming principles that they perceive have little value. Be careful to always know your audience.

3. **Emotional support**—Anger, bitterness, loneliness, unforgiveness, and low self-esteem are just a few of the common emotional issues that a single mom may face. Whether she is a first- time teen mom or a divorcée in her 40s, she must have a venue where she can express her feelings, work through her emotions, and learn to lean on Christ as her ultimate healer. We also keep a list of free or nearly-free counselors available for moms who need additional emotional support.

4. **Spiritual growth**—*Who am I in Christ? Now that I am a single mother, alone, with no support from a spouse, how can I make it? What does it mean to be a godly mother? What does it mean*

*to lean on Christ in times of crisis? How do I do that when I'm so depressed?*

These are all questions that single moms begin to ask. Many who were active in their local churches tend to fall away from attendance and activities within their church. This is the time to reach out!

**Important note: Stick to these four areas**. This is not the time to have an in-depth study on the book of Ruth or to offer deep theological teaching. When you are dealing with women who are recently divorced, are struggling with loneliness, or have had an unplanned pregnancy, what they need are practical tips in a non-preachy fashion. Please do not misunderstand what I am saying here.

Are Bible studies on Ruth, Esther, and the Proverbs 31 Woman all relevant and important? Absolutely. But the purpose of a single moms ministry to is to reach *all* single mothers. While those studies may work perfectly well for churched single moms, they could totally alienate the new Christian or unchurched single mom we are trying to reach for Christ. She may be embarrassed that she is not more knowledgeable of the Bible at her age or fear that you are preaching *at* her rather than encouraging her. Keep in mind that women who have been severely hurt through divorce or a failed relationship and have been away from church for a long time are oftentimes looking for excuses *not* to come to your support group. Therefore, I suggest keeping the biblical teachings simple and easy to understand, in order to support every single mother your ministry serves. Both mature and new Christians alike will understand and appreciate this approach in the spirit of making everyone comfortable.

For this reason, we encourage the single moms in our program to be active within the church outside of our single mothers program. We encourage them to take classes, attend Sunday School, and participate in other Bible studies. But in the context of reaching **all** single mothers (both churched and unchurched), it is best to stick to the four main areas above.

### Step 3: Purchase Overwhelmed: The Life of a Single Mom *as a resource for your new ministry*

*Overwhelmed: The Life of a Single Mom* is my first book, which chronicles in great detail my own journey through unwed pregnancy, single parenting, financial obstacles, and emotional healing. In the beginning, I was quite intimidated about promoting *Over- whelmed: The Life of a Single Mom* because I was certain people would see it as self-promotion and only an attempt to sell more books. But God gave me total freedom over that. God most assuredly gave me the book to write in an effort to reach as many single moms and broken women as possible, as well as to encourage and inspire all. I believe its contents were breathed by God and accomplish just that.

In its first six months the book has sold out numerous times across the country. It has been endorsed by major ministries, including CBN, Single Parent Family Life, and Lifeway Christian Stores, and provides an eye-opening look at the struggle of single mothers. God has opened doors for it to be endorsed by some of the largest churches in the country as well. The second half of the book, arguably the most important half, details all the things that the Lord taught me through the journey—Freedom in Christ, Parenting 101, Overcoming Abuse, Financial Stewardship, and much more. The book includes a 12-part study designed specifically for single parent small groups to foster discussion and is being used in churches across the globe. If you discover that your group needs to camp out on a topic for longer than the specified time, e.g., parenting or overcoming abuse, you will find that the book allows for such flexibility. The book allows for two meetings on Overcoming Abuse. However, when I began to teach on the subject, I found that our current group needed four lessons, so we simply divided the lessons.

I recommend that your first meeting be a "meet and greet" whereby women can get to know one another and share some small details of their lives. This is an opportunity for you to pass out the books (if your church is purchasing them for the ladies) or have the books available for purchase. Assign the *Part 1: The Autobiography* to be read before the next meeting.

### Step 4: Decide when and where to have the meetings

We recommend meeting on a weekend (Friday, Saturday, or Sunday night) for one and half hours twice monthly. We have tried several different meeting days and found this model to work best. Moms have an opportunity to wind down on the weekends and experience some "me" time. What better way to enjoy relaxation than through a single moms support group?

I do not recommend having the single moms meeting as part of the traditional Wednesday night service or Sunday morning ser-vice. The reason is three-fold:

1  Single moms who work two jobs or work and go to school will usually be unavailable during the week.

2  In addition, moms who parent older children have homework, sports practices, etc., and this is an additional reason to keep them away.

3  Sunday morning Bible study will likely intimidate the unchurched single mom who has not been in church for years (or never been in church). Again, you hear me speaking about the unchurched single mom. Saved single moms would more than likely come to the single moms support group even if you

had it at 6:00 a.m. on Tuesdays. The mature Christian understands the value of relationships and continued biblical education. If you are dealing with anger, hurt, and bitterness, however, it is best to remove as many obstacles as possible to create a warm, comfortable environment for the new moms.

Let me address the reason behind having the meeting for only 1.5 hours twice monthly. Haven't we all had the experience of being in a Bible study, corporate meeting, or party and praying for it to just be over? The event simply ran too long and our minds began wandering to all the tasks we needed to complete by day's end. A single mother's to-do list is often twice as long as others'. If she comes to the support group one time and the meeting drones on and on, she will likely not come back. She has too much to do. Her time is valuable. By contrast, if she knows that the meetings always start and end on time, she can properly plan her evening and will be more likely to return. Single moms have many responsibilities and carving out time on their things-to-do list will require great sacrifice on their parts. Be intentional about starting and ending on time and keep it short.

It is important to note that meeting with regularity allows moms to begin to network and develop relationships. Meetings more than twice a month could become too cumbersome for moms— just another thing to add to her already full plate. Groups that meet only once a month or less often do not allow enough time for the participants to develop those much-needed friendships on a genuine level. I have found meeting twice monthly to be the perfect mix between the two.

We originally met in a living room at someone's home. We only had a handful of women. We provided childcare in the back of the home. This was acceptable for a season. Before long, however, we outgrew that living room and obtained permission to meet at our church. We used classrooms at first but then outgrew them and now meet in the sanctuary. This is a great problem to have. It does not matter where you meet, but be certain that childcare is accounted for, which leads me to the next point.

### Step 5: Always provide childcare and a meal at meetings
### This point is non-negotiable.

Single moms do not have the luxury of leaving children at home with a spouse. Therefore, providing a safe and comfortable place for moms to leave their children eases the mom's anxiety and also increases your possibility for growth. We do not allow children in our meetings—*ever!* Children, ages 0–16 have a place to go within our church building that is age-ap- propriate and fun. Moms need that time to relax. They need that time to share.

We have also found that even moms who do not normally leave their children in childcare will open up and share more when they do not have a screaming toddler on their hip. (The only exception to this rule is allowing mothers who have newborns to bring their babies to the meetings.)

You may be wondering about church budget at this point. (See Chapter 8 Frequently Asked Questions for information on budgeting concerns. We have discovered some creative ways to work with any church budget, including the non-existent ones!)

In the beginning, we did not provide meals at our meetings. We would sometimes provide a light snack, but we simply did not have a budget to feed the moms. What we discovered, however, was that children were telling our childcare providers that they were hungry or had not eaten all day. Not only is providing a meal a biblical instruction (Proverbs 19:17, Matthew 25:35), it is also a blessing in many ways. Moms may not have time to prepare a meal and clean up before coming to the meeting. Providing a meal also cuts down on their grocery budget for that day, thus saving the mom money. In addition, it is a thoughtful way to provide that extra TLC that these moms desperately desire.

 **Quick tip:** An inexpensive way to make sure that all the moms are fed is to call upon other members of the congregation to assist in this area. They want to help, but some- times do not know what to do. This is a great way to give someone else an opportunity to serve as well as giving them a place of value. See Chapter 8 for more details.

## *Step 6: Diversify the message and the speakers*

While I do recommend using teaching material to provide structure to the group, it is important to allow the Holy Spirit to lead. Many times through the years I had been planning to teach the next lesson in our book and felt led to stray from that lesson for a particular meeting. Be sensitive to allowing the Holy Spirit to move and work. Perhaps a subject has arisen repeatedly in your group discussion. That is the perfect cue to implement an "off-schedule" lesson. We have seen the Holy Spirit move in great ways during those less-structured, unscheduled topics.

In addition, we have had great speakers share with our ladies from time to time. It is a special treat for our group to hear from a variety of leaders. Sometimes the special guest may be a business person from the community who can share on finances. Some-times the speaker may be a lead pastor or Bible teacher. Other times, we have had single-mom experts or parenting experts. Some of the best times we have had with guest speakers are single moms who are successfully navigating the journey and who have shared their testimony with us. Rotating lessons and speakers, breaks up any monotony the group may experience and, as I always say, "keeps them on their toes."

When broaching the subject of growth, the topic of diversifying speakers is important. Varying topics as well as speakers keeps the moms engaged and excited, as they do not want to miss what God has in store for them at the upcoming meeting.

### Step 7: Spend time with the women

What a simple but powerful point. Single moms in your group are not just a number. They are women who desire to forge lasting friendships. I have been quoted as saying, "I've had more coffees and lunches with single moms than I can even count. And I've loved every second of it." When your support group is still in its infancy, you will have time to take single moms for coffee or lunch on occasion, as your schedule permits. Be certain to get to know them. Spend time on the phone with them or emailing them. Small gestures, such as a thoughtful card, go a long way in developing relationships. As the women become connected to you and others in the group, they will come more often.

As the group grows, raising up volunteers will become more important. There is no way one person alone can effectively minister to a group of, say, 20 single moms. It's the fast track to ministry burnout—trying to do coffees, lunches, phone calls, etc., all by yourself. Be certain that these things are being done, yes, but assign leaders and volunteers to do them. Delegate! The leaders and volunteers will be happy to for the opportunity to serve, and the single moms will be especially grateful that someone took the time to notice them.

### Step 8: End each meeting with prizes and giveaways

Make it a regular part of your meetings to provide freebies at the end of the meeting. Not only does these giveaways meet a tangible need, such as clothing or food, but they give the moms some- thing to look forward to. This is a great way to reach out to the surrounding community and increase attendance. Through the years, I have been asked time and again how to obtain freebies on a limited budget. Initially, we were simply providing a few tables of hand-me-down clothes or household items (similar to a free garage sale). We soon discovered that local retail stores that are discontinuing merchandise look to churches and nonprofits to give away these items. We developed relationships with the managers of many of these stores and began to receive new items. The items may have been removed from store shelves due to a dented box or some similar "imperfection," but the items inside were not damaged. I cannot tell you how excited single moms are to receive dented boxes of perfume. We also made contact with local food banks and were able to receive large quantities of food.

We are happy to accept lightly used furniture and clothes from the community or church congregation. I make it a point to go through every item (or have a volunteer do so) to assure that the items we give away are in good condition. We want to treat our single moms with the utmost dignity and respect, as they should be treated, so we are certain not to give out items that have been too heavily used.

As time has gone by, we have given women a large array of gifts and goodies, including perfume, make-up, hair accessories, toiletries, food, clothes, diapers, baby items, and much more. It has become a wonderful highlight of our meetings. Since every meeting's giveaways are a surprise, ladies always look forward to the unveiling of the gifts.

The question may now arise, "Aren't you concerned that some ladies may be coming only to get free items?" My answer is, "Not at all!" Do I believe that it happens from time to time? Of course. But no matter the reason that a woman comes into our ministry, we are going to give her Jesus, comfort, love, and encouragement before she ever gets that free bottle of shampoo, so it is well worth it!

## Structure of the Single Moms Ministry

We have already discussed the time and frequency of the meetings, but what takes place during the actual meetings? Here are some guidelines:

- **First 30 Minutes**—Moms should be mingling and enjoying a meal together.

- **Second 30 Minutes**—Speaker shares a relevant message.

- **Last 30 Minutes**—Ladies divide into small groups (with a leader present in each group) to discuss the message, share prayer requests, and encourage fellowship.

In the beginning, our meeting structure was a bit different. We visited and shared a meal for the first 30 minutes then had our lesson and discussion for one hour. In those days, the group was still under 20 women, so the message could be stopped and started as necessary to answer questions and foster discussion. Once a group crests 20 members, we recommend having a teaching and then breaking into smaller groups to allow moms to share prayer requests and ask questions. Small groups protect the intimacy and relationship of the single moms ministry, even as the group continues to grow. Each small group will consist of a leader who will act as a facilitator of discussion. We have found that single moms (or former single moms) work best as small group facilitators, as many of the moms will feel comfortable opening up to a fellow single mom. She offers credibility and brings passion to the ministry.

2 Corinthians 1:4 says: "He comforts us in all troubles so that we can comfort others." A current single mom who is strong in her walk with the Lord or a former single mom with like standing

is ideal in providing wise counsel to current single mothers. God has been faithful to raise up key single moms within our ministry as we have grown, and the same will be true for you.

### *Managing volunteers*

Discussing the structure of the meeting leads us to managing volunteers. One of the biggest mistakes I made as a new leader was attempting to handle everything myself. My controlling nature was such that I had convinced myself that God gave me this vision of helping single moms and no one could do it as well as I. Boy, how wrong I was! Not only did I find myself exhausted in the early years of the ministry, but I grew bitter. I would complain regularly about how "no one was helping me," yet I would not *allow* anyone to help me! I was nervous that if I turned over food planning and preparation to someone else, they would forget, and the moms would go hungry. Or what if I asked someone to organize our children's program and they forgot?

It actually made me bitter. I was in full-time ministry, doing it all alone (by my own account), and was bitter. I was bitter about why more single moms would not come to the meetings. I was bitter because no one would help me.

I can only write this honestly now because I know that God has delivered me from this. My deep desire is to empower and equip those who have been called to minister to single moms and part of that process is that we all be 100% honest. I hope that my candor provides clear instruction to those who follow. As the leader of such a large ministry, it has been critical that I surround myself with volunteers who are as passionate as I am about single moms and those who will prove wonderful armor-bearers within the ministry.

As the ministry expands, you will need more volunteers. We use volunteers in the following capacities:

- Childcare
- Food Service
- Prayer Partners
- Small Group Leaders
- Clean-up and Set-up Crew
- Guest Services (a service whereby the volunteer strategically mingles to make sure that all feel comfortable and welcome)

Not only does having volunteers remove some of the weight from your shoulders, it gives others value. They have a purpose. As we have moved single moms into these roles, we have seen them become more excited about coming to meetings. They have a responsibility there and an opportunity to serve and give back. (For more on volunteer development, see Chapter 8.)

## Be ready for the harvest

As word gets out that you are giving away free items and ministering to single moms, **your single moms ministry will grow.** Many prayers through the years were from frustration that the ministry would not grow. Of course, there were several things that I learned about ministry as time went on. (Isn't that *always* God's plan?) Over time we needed to make several changes in the way we did things and adjusted to the Lord's leading and practical realities of the ministry (as outlined above), but I knew the Lord had given me visions of thousands of single moms. Yet I could not seem to get more than five or six to come faithfully to the meetings.

I felt as though I was doing everything I could to foster a desirable environment that they would want to attend. I was praying, studying, and preparing for the lessons. I was calling the women regularly, reaching out to have coffee, and emailing them to let them know we missed them when they were absent. I passed out fliers and used social media. I did simply everything I could think of. It was during my prayer time (or rather my *complaining* time) that God spoke to me and revealed to my heart this message:

> *"I cannot release all these women to you, until you are ready. It will overwhelm you."*

Here I was, frustrated and confused about what it was I was doing wrong and why the women would not attend, yet God was showing me that it was about him and his timing. Rest in knowing that. Be faithful in the small ministry.

Matthew 25:23 says, "The master said, 'Well done, my good and faithful servant. You have been faithful in handling this small amount, so now I will give you many more responsibilities. Let us celebrate together!"

Once I became comfortable in that scripture, God opened the floodgates. We had our last meeting of the semester in May of one year with only eight ladies. We took a break for that summer. Upon returning in September of that same year, we opened the doors to 75 women! In just 90 days, God did a lot of work in my own heart. I believe today that is the reason our ministry began to grow. We now host hundreds of women and have seen God's mighty hand at work through the ministry in the lives of not only our single moms but through our leaders and volunteers. I get excited all over again every time I think about all that God has done and all that He is going to do.

CHAPTER 8

# FREQUENTLY ASKED QUESTIONS

*Frequently given answers…*

E ven the most comprehensive guides often leave leaders with more ministry questions. This chapter answers some of the more common questions we receive from those who are interested in starting or growing a single moms ministry.

## How do I launch a new ministry when there is no budget available?

This is the most common question. There is no doubt that our global economy has been difficult for some time. Consequently, churches have had to fine-tune budgets. Given such constraints, starting a new ministry may not seem feasible. But the good news is that much of our ministry design costs little to no money. Consider these money-saving tips.

In the last chapter, I explained that childcare and meal provisions were non-negotiables in a single moms' ministry. But where does the money come from to pay for childcare and meals? You can solicit childcare volunteers from the church's existing youth ministry, widows' ministry, moms' group, or senior citizens class. Youth pastors are often looking for ways for their youth to serve and give back to the community. Elderly grandmothers within the church would love the opportunity to rock babies or spend time with children. In addition, married moms may want to serve in this area as a way to thank God for their spouse and show com- passion to single moms. Grieving widows may greatly value an opportunity to serve as a way to curb loneliness.

The same is true of food service. Look in the existing congregation for potential cooks for the meetings. Post "help wanted" spots in the church bulletin or newsletter and provide a sign-up sheet to rotate volunteers for upcoming meetings. Local food banks are also willing to donate food to the ministry, so in many cases it is only a matter of having someone prepare it. Pasta and casseroles are two huge crowd-pleasers that are also budget-friendly dishes. We have had meetings with a bigger turn-out than anticipated, and our food service volunteers would get together and pray over the meal that God would provide and stretch it. Never once have we had a child or mom leave hungry. God always provides.

### *What are some good places to find volunteers?*

- Youth Ministry
- Women's Ministry
- Senior Citizens
- Christian radio stations (such as K-LOVE) will advertise for free if it is a public service announcement (PSA)
- Partner with other churches
- Mothers of Pre-schoolers (MOPS)
- Widows' Ministry
- Moms' Bible Studies

### *How do we avoid burnout?*

1. ***Rest.*** Even our Creator rested in Genesis 2:3: "And God blessed the seventh day and declared it holy, because it was the day when he rested from all his work of creation."

   There is nothing wrong with taking time off. There should be balance in your life to make it healthy. Just as it is unhealthy to attend church seven days a week and neglect your family in doing so, it is unhealthy to attend to single mom's ministry seven days a week. Tasks will go undone if you immerse in ministry 24/7. Trust me when I say you will burn out and be exhausted and overwhelmed.

   In our single moms' program, we actually take off during the summer. Our semester runs simultaneous to the school year, so that the summer is a time for families to enjoy one another. This was not the case in the beginning. In the beginning, we had only been meeting for about six months and were having great success in our group. The attendance was beginning to increase, albeit only slightly. The moms were beginning to share more readily. I was certain that taking off for the entire summer would be to the detriment of our group. How wrong I was! I found that meeting continually without any sort of break, not only exhausted me, but also the ladies. We all need rest.

   We do plan an occasional get-together, but no formal meetings are held. This allows all leaders and volunteers time for rejuvenation.

2. ***Seek a mentor.*** James 5:16 says "Confess your sins to each other and pray for each other so that you may be healed. The earnest prayer of a righteous person has great power and produces wonderful results." As ministry leaders, there can be a tendency for us to "have it all together." There is an added pressure of leading others to be godly women and the

significance of that calling on our lives. We sometimes put an unnecessary burden of perfectionism on our lives. Be certain that you have someone to whom you can confess your sins, share candidly, and pray.

3. ***Recognize your role.*** As I have grown in my relationship with the Lord, my deepest desire is to have others find that same relationship. I want to turn on a light switch and have people instantly come to know him. I suppose that is the instant-fix part of us that refuses to wait patiently on God's timing. Although we have seen some of the most radical transformations of lives you can imagine in our single moms ministry, we have also seen women that we have poured into for years who are going around the same mountains, dealing with the same struggles, and living the same lifestyle. I have often wanted to scream, "Why don't you just get it?!"

Paul wrote in 1 Corinthians 3:6–9: "I planted the seed in your hearts, and Apollos watered it, but it was God who made it grow. It is not important who does the planting, or who does the watering. What is important is that God makes the seed grow. The one who plants and the one who waters work together with the same purpose. And both will be rewarded for their own hard work. For we are both God's workers. And you are God's field."

We are ***not*** God. It is not necessary for us to always see the fruit of our labor. It is necessary to keep planting the seeds. After I came to a full acceptance that I will not see every seed grow— that sometimes the seed I sow will only grow many years later— I experienced great freedom. Be aware that you will absolutely and completely exhaust yourself trying to *save* these women. That is not your job. The Holy Spirit ministers and grows. We plant. We water.

### *Can you discuss more on volunteer training and development?*

Much of our own volunteer training has been done collectively within the broader design of our church. Each church should have a healthy way of raising up and developing volunteers and leaders within the church walls, so this answer may vary a little with what you do at your church, and that is okay. Each one of the leaders in our single moms ministry (those who facilitate small group discussion) has completed introductory training, Bible education, and leadership classes. It is important that the volunteers we release into leading and mentoring other women understand biblical basics and are equipped to do the job. If a volunteer feels that she is not properly trained, she will likely quit from frustration.

In addition to the aforementioned classes, we have a continuing education program whereby leaders and volunteers complete additional refresher classes periodically. We also hold quarterly meetings with our single mom volunteer team to discuss ways to improve the ministry, to deal with problems that have arisen, and to pray for one another. It is important that all volunteers and leaders understand the vision of the ministry and the vision of the church in which they serve. This moves the body of Christ forward.

### *How do I retain volunteers and manage turnover?*

Isn't that the million-dollar question? Many of our volunteers have quit through the years for reasons as varied as the individual.

Let me share a brief story. Nora was referred to me through a mutual friend and came highly-recommended. She had gone through a bitter divorce, received counseling, and was at a healthy place in her walk with the Lord. She desperately wanted to help other single moms in their walk. I was certain that she would be perfect and because I was in such need of good volunteers, I admittedly did not do much praying and seeking. She started helping with the ministry and attended for a few months. She called me one day and began to explain that she was quitting.

"Jennifer, ever since I started volunteering with the single moms group, everything has gone wrong. My business has slowed down, so I have run into financial difficulties. My daughter was hospitalized with an illness. Some old emotions have resurfaced. I am just going to have to step down. This is too hard."

Imagine my disappointment. I was losing a volunteer, who I had believed would work out perfectly for what we were trying to accomplish. But more than that, I recognized a deeper matter. As I stated earlier, single moms support groups are "high-level ministry." We are helping to radically change lives. Make no mistake about it: Satan is none too thrilled.

When volunteers approach you about working with single moms be certain that you pray first. Be sure to inform them that being busy about our Father's business creates a target on our back. When attacks come—and they will definitely come—volunteers must be ready to persevere.

Here are a few other things that I have learned about volunteers. First, if you do not equip volunteers to do the task, they will become frustrated and leave. You must spend time in training and developing them. Second, volunteers have additional obligations, as well. Be certain that you are scheduling meetings at convenient times and are not calling meetings too often. An additional note here is to ensure that your volunteers know their value. They must know that they are genuinely cared for and that their presence makes a difference in the ministry. Whether it is scrubbing toilets, wiping baby noses, or delivering the message, each role is vitally important to the growth and health of the ministry. No role is more important than any other. Volunteers need to know they are not simply placeholders. Take the time to get to know those who serve with you.

Be certain that you are not recruiting volunteers simply to fill a position, but that you are being sensitive to the Holy Spirit's leading. God places passion within us, and there are women everywhere who are filled with compassion for single moms. Find those volunteers. The ones who have caught the vision and are passionate to see it come to fruition are the ones who will stay for the long haul. They will come in early and stay late. They view their service as an opportunity rather than an obligation.

Lastly, understand that seasons change. What worked for one season might not work for another. Volunteers move away, get married, transition from toddler years into teenage years, etc. Simply because a volunteer has decided that her season of service within the ministry is over does not mean that it is a personal attack on you.

## *How do I protect the privacy and integrity of the ministry?*

This question arises from the common concern that leaders have about creating a safe environment for single moms to share and releasing the concern that others within the group may gossip about the things shared. That could happen, of course, just as it could in any other relationship, support group, or Bible study. I have been in this ministry for years now and have worked with hundreds of single moms and I can tell you that this has been only an extremely rare occurrence. Since most of the women are so grateful to have a place to come and share, and many of their struggles are strikingly similar, we have found that there has not been this great desire to gossip outside of the group setting.

As with any ministry, however, there will be times when you will act under the authority God has given you and must take a firm line in an area. Protecting the women in the ministry is a necessity. In the event there is a breach of trust and gossiping is discovered, you must take action. Remind the moms regularly that this is a safe place to share and that you expect each member to give the same level of respect to every other member that she expects to receive (Luke 6:31). If a specific incident arises discuss it with the individual involved. Show tremendous grace but be firm in the expectation. If it is a repeated problem, then the person may need to be removed from the group for a season to protect the group. These decisions should always be discussed with the church leadership to whom you submit.

It is also important to note the importance of integrity in the ministry. Acts 24:16 says: "I always try to maintain a clear conscience before God and all people." Be certain that the environment you create has great integrity. Live above reproach. The women in the ministry are watching you and the other leaders.

It is important that you are not guilty of gossip and that they are confident that they can trust you. Our desire, as Christians, should be to continue to seek out truth and a deeper relationship with our Heavenly Father. As the women see this desire within the leadership to learn more about Christ, the hope is that they, too, will begin to seek Him and put away those things.

### How do I handle it when a leader's lifestyle is questionable?

We have all seen even well-known Christian leaders fall into sin. Why should we be surprised? Satan is actively seeking to steal, kill, and destroy (John 10:10), and certainly a ministry that is as necessary as helping hurting single mothers is on his radar. I can attest that it is extremely difficult to have those accountability discussions and even more difficult to remove a leader from her position based on her unwillingness to submit to authority or lifestyle issues.

Refer to 1 Corinthians 8:13, which says: "So if what I eat causes another believer to sin, I will never eat meat again as long as I live—for I do not want to cause another believer to stumble."

This scripture was about far more than eating meat. What we are talking about is the importance of encouraging our Chris- tian brothers and sisters in their walk with Christ. When we begin to dissect the lifestyle of leaders in the church, we are potentially talking life or death for non-believers. It is that serious. Sometimes a candid discussion with a leader about this very thing is enough for the leader to change her behavior. That is certainly the hope.

There may be occasions, however, when a leader must be removed from leadership. If this is the case, it is vitally important to the relationship and the ministry that it is handled with care.

Privacy and grace are key. The leader should be encouraged to stay connected to the church and ministry. Extend forgiveness and grace readily.

Leaders, God is so good. God does not lead us *to* what he will not lead us *through*. (If I knew who first spoke those words of wisdom, I would credit him here!) Be diligent in seeking his face first. Our desire to bring him glory will ultimately result in others' finding him. It has never been about growing a ministry for numbers' sake but rather for souls' sake!

# RECOMMENDED RESOURCES

*For more curriculum, support, training, and materials for your single moms' program, visit www.thelifeofasinglemom.com*